HEALING WORDS

30 Devotional Word Studies for Emotional and Spiritual Healing

By

Susan C. Brozek, M.S.W.,
With
Jeffrey M. Brozek

This book was produced in conjunction with:

HEALING WORD
PSYCHOTHERAPY SERVICES, LLC
Mequon, Wisconsin ♦ www.healing-word.com

Dedications

…To my precious husband, Jeff.
For your unfailing love, encouragement, and support.
You mean the world to me!
It is an honor to write this book with you.
and
…To my mother, Carol.
You are the picture of kindness, love, and generosity.
May God bless you richly for how you've blessed me.
~Susan

…To my beautiful, loving Susan.
You are the most precious princess I could have ever asked for. You
are a priceless treasure from God above – He could not have
picked out a more perfect wife for me. I am so grateful for you. I
will always love and cherish you forever!
~Jeff

…And to our wonderful, glorious Savior, Jesus Christ.
You are our Rock and our Redeemer.
To <u>*You*</u> be all the glory!
~Jeff & Susan

Table of Contents

The Authors

SUSAN C. BROZEK, M.S.W., L.C.S.W., is a licensed Christian psychotherapist. She provides professional Christian counseling services, covering the entire spectrum of mental health issues, with a special emphasis on the spiritual. Susan is the founder and director of Healing Word Psychotherapy Services, LLC, located in Mequon, Wisconsin. (For contact information, please visit her website at *www.healing-word.com*). She has spoken at many state-wide conferences, workshops, and seminars, and she also hosted a year-long weekly radio program called "Healing of the Mind", presenting a Christian perspective on mental health and psychological issues. Susan is an active member of several national professional associations, and she also does volunteer work for a Milwaukee-based charitable healthcare organization.

Susan has been called to a ministry of healing. Her passion is to bring God's healing touch to the wounded, the broken-hearted, and the discouraged. As a standard in her practice, Susan maintains that God is the true Source of healing and transformational power in an individual's life. She is recognized for her sensitive integration of scriptural truths and psychological principles. Her vision is to see the healing truth of God's love set captives free.

Susan graduated from Purdue University with her Bachelor's

degree in Psychology, and she received her Master's degree from the University of Wisconsin-Milwaukee. She and her husband Jeff reside in Whitefish Bay, Wisconsin, with their two Golden Retrievers, Morgan and Chester.

JEFFREY M. BROZEK is a committed Christian and husband, and has a Bachelor's degree in Electrical Engineering from Purdue University (where he met his beautiful wife and received the Lord) and received his Master's degree in the same field from the University of Wisconsin-Madison. It was through these programs that he has learned the disciplines of study, cultivated a passion for learning (not to mention the passion he has for his wife, first and foremost!), and has now applied those disciplines and passion to the study of God's word. He is a strong defender of marriage and of the faith, and firmly believes in, and is committed to, the integrity of both.

As such, he, along with his wife, seek God's wisdom concerning the role of the spiritual dimensions in our earthly lives, seek to expose the lies of darkness, and continue to search the deeper things of God "into which angels long to look" (1 Peter 1:12).

Jeff and his wife Susan have been called as a ministry team, and they direct a healing prayer ministry at their home church in Port Washington, Wisconsin, called "Lifeline Ministries." They also hold many seminars together on spiritual and emotional healing issues.

Introduction

But the centurion said, "Lord, I am not worthy for You to
come under my roof, but just say the word,
and my servant will be healed."
~ Matthew 8:8 ~

J ust speak the word—this was the only thing that the centurion
requested. The story of the Roman centurion is one with which
many of us are likely familiar. It was an act of faith on the part of
the centurion for he knew that Jesus had the authority to heal his
servant. The centurion came to Jesus because He knew that only He
could speak a *healing word* on behalf of his servant.

Jesus continues to speak His healing words to His children
today through the Holy Spirit and through His Holy Word, the
Bible. John's gospels tells us that Jesus Christ is the Word (see John
1:1-18), and since He is, we can trust that His words will be the
right words for our healing. If we look at the original Greek word
for "healed" in Matthew 8:8, it is the word *iaomai*, which means *to
cure, to restore to health, to heal, or to make whole.* It carries with it
the idea of a full and total healing of a particular ailment or condition. It is also important to note that the centurion possessed and
expressed his faith in Jesus *prior* to his servant being healed. It is

quite clear that most of the accounts of healing in the gospels were instances where faith was already present on the part of the individuals seeking a healing touch from Jesus *before* they were healed. Faith is not a power which causes the healing to occur; rather, it is *preparation* for God's healing power. Thus Jesus, who speaks life with His Words, can bring healing and freedom to us in our place of need as we express our faith in Him and His healing power.

This healing is beyond physical and medicinal only. In fact, another Greek word meaning "to heal", is *therapeuo* and of its 43 occurrences in the New Testament, only 2 refer to healing by ordinary medical means. In all the other passages, it refers to the miraculous healings performed by Jesus or His disciples. Further yet, anyone healed by Jesus is a person that is healed in their entire being by the word of the Messiah. Acts 10:38 states, "You know of Jesus of Nazareth, how God anointed Him with the Holy Spirit and with power, and how He went about doing good and healing all who were oppressed by the devil, for God was with Him." Jesus healed (*iaomai*) all who were oppressed by the devil. The word for oppressed carries with it the idea of being tyrannized, ruled over, or being worn down. *Therefore, Jesus not only heals us physically, He heals us from the weights that drag and wear us down!*

The Old Testament is also filled with examples of the Lord's healing. We can see this in Psalm 107:20 where the psalmist says, "He sent His word and healed them, and delivered them from their destructions." Here, the Hebrew word for "healed" is the word *rapha* which conveys the meanings of *to heal, to restore to normal, to cure, and to mend*. It becomes clear from a reading of the Old Testament that it is a characteristic of faith in the Lord that He alone is the source of all our healing, because all aspects of our lives are dependent upon the Lord alone. This verse, like the one in Matthew, also links healing with God's Word. Of course, there are countless other means by which God can bring about healing in our lives; however, we've decided to focus upon His Holy Word and the healing that it can bring about.

Since there are many different areas of our lives that may need healing, this devotional book will focus on the application of God's Word concerning the aspects of emotional and spiritual healing.

Since everyone is born into this world spiritually dead and in need of a Savior, in addition to the effects of a sinful world and our own sinful choices upon our lives, it's quite clear that we all need both God's spiritual and emotional healing. Our spiritual healing begins with our spirits being born again (see John 3:3-7) and continues as we mature in Christ and begin to receive His healing for our emotional wounds. So often, we as Christians don't expect enough from God. In fact, some people think that the current condition they're in is all God has for them in life; this is not true! As such, this book is for those who want to seriously participate in their own healing process. *True healing is a <u>journey</u> much more than it is a mere destination.* It can also be painful at times, and for this reason some may shy away from entering in to this life-changing process. But we encourage you to stretch your trust and faith in God, and permit Him to gently guide you as you examine your heart and allow Him to apply His healing balm to your soul and spirit through these word studies. Jesus' healing truth brings freedom to your life!

Since God is the true source of healing in our lives and He often heals through His Word (whether through reading or application), our intent is to bring His Word to you and then begin to dig out some of the deeper meanings in His Word. Thus, each devotional word study will begin with a verse followed by a section titled "**<u>The Words BEHIND the Word</u>**". We've given you a little taste of this already as we delved into the original Hebrew or Greek words used in the ancient manuscripts of the Bible. From there, we bring a practical application of the word to further aid in your understanding. This section is titled "**<u>Now That I Know It, How Do I Live It?</u>**", and is meant to aid in applying God's truth to the areas of our lives that need emotional and spiritual healing.

As Susan knows in her private practice as a clinical psychotherapist, she is a vessel that is used by God and the true healing comes from <u>Him</u>. In fact, one of the Greek words for healing is *therapeia*, and one of its derivatives is where we get our English word for "therapy". The meaning that it stresses is the medical service, or the care and attention that are given during the healing process which then results in healing. Therefore, as Susan is preparing for her clients, researching relevant issues, and engaging in therapy, she is aiding in the healing process that God is ultimately accomplishing in that particular individual. In much the same way, our prayer as the authors of this book is that through the research and application of God's Word, He will use this devotional to bring about a greater measure of His healing in your life!

Jehovah Rapha...
The Lord Our Healer

*And He said, "If you will give earnest heed to the voice of the
LORD your God, and do what is right in His sight, and give ear to
His commandments, and keep all His statutes, I will put none of
the diseases on you which I have put on the Egyptians;
for I, the LORD, am your healer."*
~ Exodus 15:26~

Author Ann Spangler in her book *"Praying the Names of God"*,
explains the meaning of the powerful word, "rapha", as one of
God's Names:

> "The Hebrew word *'rapha'* means *'heal'*, *'cure'*,
> *'restore'*, or *'make whole'*. Shortly after His people
> left Israel for the Promised Land, God revealed
> himself as *Jehovah Rapha*, 'the LORD who heals.'
> The Hebrew Scriptures indicate that God is the
> source of all healing. As you pray to Jehovah Rapha,
> ask Him to search your heart. Take time to let Him
> show you what it contains. If He uncovers any sin,

ask for His forgiveness and then pray for healing. The New Testament reveals Jesus as the Great Physician, ***the healer of body and soul***, whose miracles point to the Kingdom of God. The verb from which *rapha* is derived occurs 67 times in the Old Testament. Though it often refers to physical healing, it usually has a larger meaning as well, involving the entire person. Rather than merely healing the body, ***Jehovah Rapha heals the mind and soul as well.***"

Spangler includes a prayer which acknowledges God as *Jehovah Rapha*, the LORD Our Healer:

"Jehovah Rapha, I bow before you today to acknowledge that you are not only my Creator but the LORD who heals me. Please heal me today, body and soul, and do the same for my loved ones. I pray that you will heal whatever is bitter in my life, transforming me in ways that glorify you. Amen."

**Let this be your prayer as well,
as you begin to take in God's *HEALING WORDS* for your life.
Jehovah Rapha is present with you on your healing journey!**

How To Use This Book

"*Healing Words: 30 Devotional Word Studies for Emotional and Spiritual Healing*" can be used as a 30-day devotional book, by reading one "healing word" per day and meditating on it, or it can be read through in one sitting. The authors' recommendation is that you, the reader, go through this book day-by-day for a month, and meditate upon God's wisdom and healing contained in each writing. The second half of this book is a lined Journal in which each of the 30 words are recorded in the same order as they appear in the first half of the book (one word for every 2 pages), along with a question to help you begin to meditate upon and consider the riches contained in God's *"Healing Words."* You may also want to invite the Holy Spirit in to bring fresh insight and revelation to you during your time of study, meditation, journaling, and prayer.

May God pour out His blessings upon you as you seek Him and allow Him to work His healing in your heart and in your life!

day #1 compassion
compassion

compassion

Bless the LORD, O my soul, and forget none of His benefits; who pardons all your iniquities, who heals all your diseases; who redeems your life from the pit, who crowns you with lovingkindness and compassion;
~ Psalm 103:2-4 ~

...<u>The Words BEHIND the Word</u>...

W hen we think of the word compassion, what most often comes to mind? Well, very likely we might think of a deep inward feeling of care, concern or even pity towards another person. In fact, the Greek word for compassion, *splangnizomai*, comes from the word *splangna* which is the word for *the intestines, the inward parts, or the bowels* which tells us that compassion really is a deep feeling inside of us. In many accounts of the Gospels, we are told that Jesus *felt* compassion for those that were flocking to see Him and He would often minister to and heal them out of that compassion. This word is also used in the story of the prodigal son in Luke 15:21 where, "his father saw him and felt compassion for him and ran and embraced him and kissed him." We can notice once again that this compassion is a feeling; however, it doesn't have to stop there...it can also move us to action.

David tells us in Psalm 103 that one of God's benefits towards us is His compassion. His compassion actually "crowns" us, which is from the Hebrew word *atar* meaning *to encircle as in attack or protection, to crown or give a crown.* If we look further into this verse, "compassion" is the word *racham* whose root meaning is *to fondle, to cherish* and thus means *compassion, pity, or mercy* or it can mean *the bowels* as well. Interestingly, the word also means *the womb,* for it is place whereby the fetus is cherished. When we bring this all together, we see that God *surrounds us with His protection and cherishes us lovingly as a baby is nurtured and protected in the womb of its mother.*

So just how is compassion relevant to our healing? One of the things we can ascertain from this is the level of God's healing that we need. If we go through life and tend to feel, or not feel as the case may be, indifference rather than compassion towards others, then we likely have hardened our hearts in some way. This hardening, which comes either due to our own sin or due to walls we've built to shield us from the hurtful sins of others, tends to block the flow of compassion from our hearts. Just as a dry riverbed soaks up what little water flows during a drought, so will hardened hearts quench God's living water. If we remember what Jesus said in John 7:38, "from his innermost being will flow rivers of living water", we can see the connection to compassion. To begin to move past this, we need to recognize that the Lord is compassionate toward us, and that at the times we need it, He wants to nurture and protect us because of the deep feelings He has towards us. As we recognize this, we will begin to experience His love in a greater measure which then softens and heals our hearts. Then, as we begin to be moved with compassion by letting God's river flow, He will continue to supply us with even more of His compassion for He knows we can only give out what He has poured into us. Let's decide today to be a seeker of, and a conduit for, God's compassion!

...Now That I Know It, How Do I Live It?...

...*compassion*

Compassion helps to heal people. When a hurting person knows that someone genuinely cares, the walls of our defenses crumble a bit and we begin to let that person "in". In a sense, we take a risk to be a little bit more vulnerable to another when we believe that someone is demonstrating true compassion, care, and concern to us and to our situation. Christ demonstrated compassion perfectly. In fact, because He is God, He knew exactly what a person needed before they even had to voice it to Him. Although this isn't necessarily possible for us as human beings to know (unless the Lord chooses to give us a word of knowledge or some other insight into what a person is struggling with), we can still show compassion to others... by looking into their eyes—the "eye gates", which truly are the window to the soul—and by listening to them tell their story, and providing encouraging feedback along the way. Sometimes a simple act like this can mean the world to someone who is hurting.

Part of what I emphasize when I meet with my clients is to truly attempt to see their pain from their viewpoint, so that I can better provide the compassion that they so desperately need. Many times, and for many people, no one has bothered to take the time and concern to show that they care. This is more devastating than we might realize, because when a person's life has been lived without being shown compassion, one of the most basic of human emotional needs, a part of them "dies" inside. In a sense, they lose hope to a degree that maybe they aren't really worthy of anyone truly caring about them. When a person reaches this point, it becomes easier for them to shut down than to keep trying, which is a very sad and dangerous place to be. At this point, walls can be built in their heart, consciously or subconsciouly. And once walls are built, they are fairly difficult to tear down on one's own. Often Christ's healing truth is needed during prayer, and potentially even deliverance, if the walls have been allowed to stay in place for long periods of time. We need to be careful about trying too hard to protect ourselves from pain, because the walls we erect as a fortress can soon turn into a prison. It's always best to put our trust in God for the protection of our heart and our emotional and psychological needs.

So as we become aware of the strong need that people have of compassion, we can then ask the Lord to show us ways in which to demonstrate it to His precious children. If we can help another feel safe and cared about, they will have much less need to try to build up their own walls to keep pain out, and they can take comfort and solace in the fact that someone else relates to what they've gone through as well.

day #2 contentment

contentment

*Not that I speak from want, for I have learned to be content
in whatever circumstances I am.*
~ Philippians 4:11 ~

…The Words BEHIND the Word…

The Apostle Paul tells us in the book of Philippians that he has learned to be content in whatever situation he was facing. This may seem quite remarkable to us especially if we consider that the Apostle likely wrote this letter during his first imprisonment in a Roman jail. In the above verse, Paul uses the Greek word *autarkes* which, in English, means "content." It is an adjective that describes Paul's condition. It is formed from the word *autos*, which means *himself*, and *arkeo*, which has the meaning of *to suffice, be sufficient, or to have sufficient strength*. Thus, it means to be self-sufficient—in a good sense! This word really conveys the idea that one has made the inward choice to be sufficient—or content—and that choice is independent of one's circumstances. The Apostle Paul had been through both times of plenty and times of lack. It was through these circumstances that he learned to be content. Here, the word for "learned" is *manthano* and it is defined quite simply as *to learn*. It carries with it the more specific meaning of *to learn by use and practice*. Another interesting observation is that the Apostle uses the 'active voice' (in Greek), which means he is the one doing the learning, and he uses the past tense whereby he says that he learned this at a specific point in time (called the 'aorist' verb tense in Greek). If we bring this all together, the Apostle Paul is indicating that he, through use and practice, has come to the point where he has learned, whatever the circumstance, to be content by making the inward choice to find sufficiency.

Another word for contentment is seen in the book of 1 Timothy 6:6, where the Apostle Paul states, "But godliness actually is a means of great gain when accompanied by contentment." In this verse, the word for "contentment" is *autarkeia*, and it is very similar in meaning to *autarkes* mentioned above. Here, it also communicates the meaning of *a satisfied mind or disposition*. The words for "great gain" convey the idea of *a large gain or acquisition*. So therefore, if we can maintain an attitude of contentment by choosing to find sufficiency, and while pursing godliness, this will result in a "large acquisition" to our spiritual growth and maturity! Achieving spiritual maturity is essential to our healing process, and contentment is one of the means that the Lord uses to bring about healing in our lives.

...<u>Now That I Know It, How Do I Live It?</u>...
...*contentment*

Comparison is a sure-fire way to lose our contentment. We can end up causing ourselves much unneeded turmoil by constantly looking to those around us and then evaluating ourselves based on our assessment of them. Part of our emotional and spiritual maturity is accepting—and even embracing—the lot we have in life, including what we look like, what we own, where we live, and so forth. We can also slip into an "it's never enough" mentality in regards to our earthly possessions and treasures. This can be an easy trap to fall into, as the media does a stellar job of creating reasons why we should all buy the latest "such-and-such", and they play on our emotional reactions in order to reel us in. We need to reach a point where we are fully content with what we possess, and to add anything further to that will only serve to complicate our lives and cause us to lose our peace.

Simply put, some things in life cannot be changed to suit our liking, and if we try to change them, it can end up backfiring on us. Just as the "Serenity Prayer" states:

> "Lord, grant me the serenity to accept the things I cannot change, the courage to change the things I can, and the wisdom to know the difference."

It is always best that a person be a "first-class" him/herself, rather than a "second-class" someone else. God created each of us from a unique blueprint meant only for us, and as soon as we allow ourselves to become dissatisfied with His creation, we open the door to unhappiness and disappointment.

Along the same lines, there are many times in life when we cannot change the circumstances that surround us. We have two choices at this juncture: we can struggle and strive and battle our way through to try to change them, or, we can merely accept them as they are. It's clear that the only decision that will bring peace to our soul is the latter; turmoil will be the by-product of the former. We can freely choose our reaction to our circumstances, even though we can't always choose our circumstances themselves. When we choose to respond with contentment, and put all of our cares into the Lord's arms, we have made the healthiest choice we can.

day #3 **forgiveness**

forgiveness

My heavenly Father will also do the same to you, if each of you
does not forgive his brother from your heart.
~ Matthew 18:35 ~

…The Words BEHIND the Word…

Matthew 18:35 is the concluding statement from the parable of the unmerciful servant. This servant, who was pardoned of a large debt that he owed his master (much like the sin debt we owe to God), did not pardon or forgive his fellow servant who owed him a small debt. Thus, he was handed over to the tormentors until he could pay back his debt. In the same way, we too can experience some type of "torment" if we do not forgive from our hearts. Now, God is not out to "torment" us; rather, He is in the business of bringing about our healing and restoration. As such, one interpretation of this passage is that it is more of a warning to us as believers as to what we should abstain from – unforgiveness. Forgiveness clearly is something God wants us to do – unforgiveness is clearly something the enemy wants us to harbor.

The expression "handed him over"—found in Matthew 18:34—is the Greek word *paradidomi*, which is compounded from the words *para* meaning *near, to the side of, or over to*, and *didomi* meaning *to give*. Therefore, it essentially means *to deliver or give over to the power of someone else.* This 'someone else' is the torturer or tormentor, whose core meaning is rooted in the word *basanizo*, which has the meaning of *to torture, harass, afflict with pain or bring about adverse circumstances.* Why would God do this? Well, because we are remaining in sin when we do not forgive and this gives the enemy of our souls a "legal right" to harass us. In addition, our own unforgiveness can result in bitterness and resentment. What happens when we've developed bitterness in our lives? Hebrews 12:15 says, "See to it that . . . no root of bitterness springing up causes trouble, and by it many be defiled", so we see that this bitterness leads to a defilement which comes from the word *miaino*. *Miaino* has the basic meaning of *staining with color as in the staining of glass*, and therefore means *to pollute, to defile.* As we look further into this passage, bitterness is rooted in the word *pikros* which was used to describe the fruit of a bitter gourd that was so bitter, it was actually viewed as a *type of poison!* Wow! We can now see how destructive unforgiveness can be, as it not only permits the enemy to afflict us, but this poisonous root forms in us and stains who we are and who God means for us to be!

Therefore, just as we need an antidote for a poisonous snake bite, we also need God's antidote of forgiveness in our lives. Forgiveness is the word *aphiemi* which is from the words *apo* meaning *away from* and *hiemi* meaning *to send.* Therefore it means *to send away from, to let go from one's possession.* Now, this sending away is not just lip service – it requires a true release from the heart. There is such a healing release when we forgive! We can see that as we obey God and extend forgiveness to others, we let the offense go away from our hearts along with the poisonous bitterness that stains us – this is truly freeing!

...Now That I Know It, How Do I Live It?...
...forgiveness

Unforgiveness is one of the biggest roadblocks to healing that I see in people's lives at my practice every day. When one of us has been hurt, and a spirit of offense can then be allowed to gain entry, it becomes a very difficult battle to truly forgive an unjust wrongdoing that we perceive as being done to us. Forgiveness is so important in our Christian walk and relationship to others that it is mentioned over and over again in Scripture. I believe that by harboring an attitude of unforgiveness in our heart, we are really hurting ourselves, not the person who has offended us. They can be proceeding on with their life as usual, while we are held in bondage by what they did to us. This is why I tend to help clients view forgiveness as a "selfish" act. This may sound unconventional, but in essence, we are the ones who benefit when we choose to forgive. The burden lifts off of us, not the other party. We can then walk in freedom as we release that person to God. And we need to keep in mind as well that although we have let the person off "our hook", they are still on "God's hook", and He will deal with them in His timing.

I also believe that a link exists between forgiveness and joy. When we make the daily choice (and yes, it usually is a daily choice!) to walk in forgiveness, we aren't weighed down by relational struggles and have a higher level of freedom as a result. When we walk freely in the Lord, joy is easier to recognize and embrace, because we are relatively unencumbered. Of course it is still possible to have joy even when dealing with unforgiveness, but I personally don't believe we can experience it to the same extent. Also, our healing process is aided greatly by our willingness to forgive an offending party, which also links with the joy we experience.

Some people—and situations—in life will be easier to forgive than others; that much is a given. But God provides exactly the right amount of strength and grace to forgive even the most egregious offense. And He will provide untold blessings for us as well when we are obedient to forgive. A quick "rule of forgiveness" is: to forgive quickly, to forgive often, and to always forgive from the heart. If we can put these suggestions into practice, we will experience God's healing power in our lives in its full measure.

day #4 truth

truth

And you will know the truth, and the truth will make you free.
~ John 8:32 ~

...The Words BEHIND the Word...

Knowing God's truth is one of the most important, if not *the* most important, endeavor we can undertake during our lives. If we never knew and believed God's truth, then we would not be saved and would despairingly miss experiencing His joy and love in Heaven. By believing and knowing God's truth, we have crossed over from death to life, from darkness to light, and from chains to freedom. Jesus told us that the truth will set us free. So, how does it set us free and how does this promote healing? Since all truth comes from God, and His word is truth (see John 17:17), let's dig further into His word and see what we can discover.

Aletheia is the word for truth in John 8:32, and it is rooted in the words *a*, meaning *not*, and *letho*, meaning *to hide*. So *aletheia* can be defined as *that which is not hidden, truth, or unveiled reality*. In ancient Greek, one of the uses of the word meant "that which is true" in contrast to "how something appears." Quite often, our perception of an event, which may or may not be based upon reality, affects our reaction to it. It *appears* to be true to us, but in reality, our *perception* has caused the truth to be *hidden*!

The Hebrew word for truth, *emeth*, is rooted in the word *aman* which carries the idea of *that which builds up or supports, makes firm* and therefore *emeth* is defined as *truth, certainty, or faithfulness*. It is the truth that forms a firm foundation for our lives and provides us with support and certainty...and it is the basis on which true healing occurs. This is exemplified in Jesus who *is* the Truth (see John 14:6). On the contrary, we surely know how lies and those things which are hidden cause a relationship to be built upon very loose footing, which can result in all types of hurt. Therefore, coming to a correct perception of reality which is based upon truth, God's truth, will bring about a firmness and stability in our lives.

Now then, how does God's truth bring about His healing? This is done by *knowing* His truth. In John 8:32, the word translated "know" is the Greek word *ginosko* and it conveys the idea of *knowing, coming to know, experiencing, or gaining the knowledge of*. There is another Greek word that is translated "know" and it is the word *oida,* which also means *to know, to have knowledge of*, and it comes from a root word meaning *to see with perception*. This word has a fundamental meaning of intuitive knowledge. In other words, as we go through the *ginosko* process of experiencing or gaining knowledge about something, and we complete this process, we now have *oida* knowledge whereby we see and understand clearly, and can now base future actions, reactions, etc. on that knowledge. That's how God's truth frees us—by experiencing Jesus' truth about a situation, our false perception becomes eradicated because we now see it from His perspective. We are now healed and free from that which bound us!

...<u>Now That I Know It, How Do I Live It?</u>...

...truth

Jesus is the Way, the Truth, and the Life. We have heard this verse many times, but let's focus right now on the Lord being our Truth. We have to know—*experientially* know (heart knowledge, not just head knowledge)—the truth, in order to spot the counterfeits. And Christ warns us that in these last days that many will be led astray, and even the elect will be deceived. So how are we to prevent ourselves from becoming one of the many who will fall into deception and falsehood?

The U.S. Mint trains its employees to spot counterfeit bills *by having them study, re-study, and re-study again the real ones*. This is exactly the approach we should use when Scripture instructs us to be discerning of spirits, because if we aren't intimately familiar with the characteristics, qualities and attributes of our King, we could very easily be fooled by satan who masquerades as an "angel of light." This is why it is so critical that we know God and know His Word! We can know God by spending time in prayer, along with spending time in His presence worshipping Him. And we need to know His Word by reading, studying, and memorizing it. Yes, these are spiritual *disciplines*, meaning that we will, at times, need to motivate ourselves to spend time with God and time in His Word even though we may not necessarily feel like it, but we will grow stronger in Him in the process. And this is the way to become acquainted with Him as The Truth!

God's Truth is the *only* Truth. I see this time and time again as I use healing prayer with clients who have been severely emotionally wounded or abused, and when we ask the true Lord Jesus Christ to minister to a person, He will provide them with a healing truth so powerful—and so specifically tailored to right where that person is in their own life—that to this day I never cease to be amazed. What may take a person years to resolve on their own, the Lord can do completely and instantaneously through His healing truth, which dispels all the lies of the enemy that may have been holding a person captive for years under false belief systems. Praise His name!

day #5 freedom
freedom

It was for freedom that Christ set us free; therefore keep standing firm and do not be subject again to a yoke of slavery.
~ Galatians 5:1 ~

...The Words BEHIND the Word...

Freedom – it is a word that many Americans hold dear to their hearts, as this country was founded upon the tenets that her people should be free. Sadly though, this freedom does not ring true for many in other parts of the world, as they are held under bondage by an oppressive government, and as such, they desire freedom. Still, freedom does come with an obligation of responsibility and it is not something that we should take for granted...and this includes our spiritual, as well as our physical, freedom.

In Galatians 5:1, the Apostle Paul tells us that, "It was for freedom that Christ set us free." The Greek words for "freedom" and "set us free" both have their root in the word *eleutheros* which has the meaning of *free, capable of movement, or unconstrained*. In classical Greek, this word had more do with political freedom like the kind of freedom we have in this country. However, the New Testament goes beyond this "worldly" definition, and presents to us a more "spiritual" definition. During Jesus' ministry, many Jews were looking for political freedom from the Romans; unfortunately, many of them were unaware of the spiritual bondage that they had to *sin*, since they believed they could be justified before God by observing the law, and it is God's law that reveals our sin problem. It is from this spiritual sin problem that Christ has set us free – He made us capable of movement, free and no longer held or entangled by the power of sin. This entanglement (translated "to be subject to") is the word *enecho* which is from *en*, meaning *in* and *echo* meaning *to have or to hold,* so it literally means *to have a hold in something, to continually possess it, or to be entangled or subject to something*. This hold is a yoke or *zugos* of bondage which is literally *something which binds or couples any two things together*! Just as two oxen are coupled together with a yoke – where one goes, the other goes – when one stops, the other stops – this is what sin tries to do us when we give in to it! Christ has set us free from the power of sin – we need to choose to walk in it! The freedom Christ purchased for us isn't really freedom until we <u>choose</u> to continually abstain from sin and give ourselves completely over to God.

This leads us to the Christian paradox of freedom – that we are free to be slaves of God. In a nutshell, Christ sets us free so that we would no longer be in bondage to sin, but now, freed from the power of sin, we can freely serve God as His bondservant. Free to be a slave to God? Isn't that a contradiction? Well, no, because when we are being obedient to God and following Him, we will remain free, as it is sin that tries to enslave us. It is when we offer ourselves to God as His slaves that we experience true freedom and healing in our lives, because God is now able to release, free up and let loose, that potential He has placed in our lives. There is no greater healing place than to be living out our God-given potential! That is true freedom – true freedom indeed!

...Now That I Know It, How Do I Live It?...

...freedom

When a person is set free physically, heavy chains have been broken off of him, restraints have been removed, cords have been cut, weights around his ankles have been taken off, and he is now *physically* free to walk, run, and do as he chooses with his physical body. But this is just a description of physical freedom. What does it mean to be free emotionally, or spiritually?

I view emotional and spiritual freedom as being rid of the baggage that can go along with each. We carry emotional baggage in the forms of past childhood hurts or abuse, broken relationships, unmet needs and expectations, along with many more such issues. Spiritual baggage can be seen as entry points that the enemy has gained into our lives through one of a number of permissible ways, including unrepented-of generational sin, family line assignments or curses, dabbling in occultic-type practices, engaging in self-destructive behaviors, just to name a few. Just because we are saved, does not mean that our "baggage" automatically disappears at salvation. Baggage is seen more as a part of the process of sanctification, which is the life-long journey to becoming more and more like Christ. After we get saved, I personally believe that sooner rather than later, we should also deal with the emotional and spiritual baggage as well, so that the necessary issues can be brought before the Lord for His healing and, as needed, deliverance. Experiencing freedom in this sense is typically an ongoing process most of the time (although there are also many times when the Lord will instantly heal us or deliver us). Some have said that the Lord is a Lord of the journey, not merely the destination, and I believe this to be the case. Christ is interested in our heart attitude as we go through the issues of life, and "work out our salvation", as Scripture states. While the human tendency is to want to "arrive", or to reach the destination as soon as possible, the Lord's agenda is sometimes different, for our own benefit so that we can learn more along the way!

It's also important to remember that yes, as Christians, we

definitely do have much freedom, but this freedom does come with parameters, or boundaries, as well. Freedom to act in chaos or mayhem or in a disruptive, disorderly manner would certainly not bring glory to God, so we need to keep in mind as well that we should respect the loving parameters that the Lord sets around our freedom for our own best interests. In a sense, we are "free not to sin", because when one sins, it actually leads to bondage, and we then become *slaves* to sin. This is exactly what the Lord Jesus has set us free from—the power of sin!

day #6 restoration

restoration

*He restores my soul; He guides me in the paths of righteousness
for His name's sake.*
~ Psalm 23:3 ~

...The Words BEHIND the Word...

Psalm 23 is perhaps the most beloved Psalm because in it we see the loving care of our Heavenly Father. A whole book could be written about this Psalm (and in fact, many have), but we want to focus here on how God brings restoration to our souls. In order for this restoration process to take place, we must first acknowledge that we are in need of restoration. In the Isaiah prophecy of Jesus in chapter 61, we are told that Jesus came "to bind up the broken-hearted." The expression "broken-hearted" comes from the Hebrew words *shavar* which means *to break into pieces, to shatter, to burst, to smash,* and from the word *lev* which refers not only to the physical heart, but also means *the innermost being, the emotions.* The word for "bind" is the word *chavash* which has a fundamental meaning of *to wrap firmly,* and thus means *to bind up, to bandage, to wrap around.* Therefore, one of Jesus' missions is take those broken pieces of our heart and soul, those parts that have been shattered and left wounded, and to wrap them firmly with His bandages of love and to bring His healing!

What happens when Jesus does this healing? He brings restoration to our souls. This restoration is from the word *shuv* which has a plentiful usage in the Old Testament and it is defined as *to turn back, to turn around, to return, to restore, or to refresh.* The basic meaning is to move back to the point from where one came. As we go through life, we experience many different kinds of hurts which attempt to bring us down and potentially cause us to view life more negatively. God's goal is to bring us back to the point we were before we experienced the hurt, and in a strange paradox, we now actually become stronger in the end, as perhaps we realized that our hearts had been held together by our own "glue." However, when God restores our hearts with His "glue", it produces a stronger and lasting bond because it is based upon trusting in His love and goodness.

If we truly desire God's healing in our lives, then we must be willing to turn back to Him. In Jeremiah 29:13 the Lord says, "You will seek Me and find Me when you search for Me with all your heart." As we turn to the Lord, He will respond by bringing restoration to those shattered pieces of our heart. Our responsibility is to offer those pieces to Him, as they will never bring themselves back together again on their own. The old adage that says "time heals all wounds" is really a misnomer – it is *God* who heals all wounds, so let's take the pieces of our heart to Him today – all of the pieces.

...Now That I Know It, How Do I Live It?...

...*restoration*

I truly believe that it is God's best for us as His children to be brought to a place of restoration and wholeness in our soul. This does not mean that we will be *perfectly* restored this side of eternity, but the Lord desires for us to be whole, and to be active in the healing process that He offers. The processes of restoration and healing are just that—processes. I subscribe to the belief that life is much more about the journey than the destination. For most of us, we'd like to "arrive", to reach our goal and our destination and know that we've made it; but God is much more interested in our heart attitude and our growth in Him along the way!

When we are willing to submit to God's process of restoration in our lives, we need to be aware that it is rarely an easy, pain-free proposition. But if we truly desire it and commit to seeking God throughout, He will bless us above and beyond anything we could've ever asked or imagined! I see this reality played out many times a day in my counseling practice; the Lord rewards those who are willing to do this hard and often painful work. There is a cost involved when we seek healing and restoration; we can't just expect to sit back and enjoy the ride without investing anything on our end. But if we don't contribute to our own process of restoration, we will miss out on God's very best for us. Yes, we may still experience some level of healing, but it will fall short of all that God desires for us to have. God never overrides our free will, so in a sense, we set the parameters for how far we're willing to let God take us in the restoration process. Some of us are very afraid of what might happen once we open the proverbial "Pandora's Box"—but in my experience with clients, I've found that their *fear* of opening the box—or of going places that potentially could contain a lot of unhealed pain—is often worse than actually facing the contents of the box itself. The enemy, of course, doesn't want us to experience healing in our lives; he'd much prefer that we remain where we're at and stick with the status quo, so that we will continue to walk around with open, unhealed and infected wounds. Once those wounds get healed through God's power, satan may lose his legal right to affect a person's life, because oftentimes when an emotional mess is cleaned up, the enemy must flee, since his "territory" has now been taken away!

We need to keep in mind as well that the Holy Spirit is a "gentleman"; He will never force us to face something that we're not ready to. He may gently nudge us in a certain direction to get our attention at times, but He waits until we align our will with His before He takes action to restore. And once we agree to let Him take us through this process, we can absolutely know and trust that He will provide us with all the grace that we'll need to deal with these painful and difficult issues. Our God is faithful, and we can count on that promise! As the well-known saying goes, "The Lord won't take you where His grace can't keep you."

day #7 # comfort
comfort

Blessed be the God and Father of our Lord Jesus Christ, the Father of mercies and God of all comfort, who comforts us in all our affliction so that we will be able to comfort those who are in any affliction with the comfort with which we ourselves are comforted by God.
~ 2 Corinthians 1:3-4 ~

...The Words BEHIND the Word...

There are a number of different means whereby we receive the comfort of God, and by digging into God's word, we can gain further insight into this concept. In the verses above, the noun form, *paraklesis*, and the verb form, *parakaleo,* are used for the words that are translated *comfort*. These words are taken from *para* meaning *along side, near, or to the side of* and *kaleo* meaning *to call.* Thus, it literally means *to call someone to come along side and be near,* and when we desire to be comforted, that is exactly what we want – someone to come near to us and offer us words of encouragement since true comfort cannot come from ourselves. Interestingly, *kaleo* has a further meaning in classical Greek where it meant *to speak to another in order that the other might be closer, either physically or in relationship.* Therefore, when we call to God for His comfort, we actually become closer to God in the process!

It's also important to remember that we have to do the calling – God is willing to comfort us, but He wants us to express our need and desire of Him to come nearer to us.

Now, we must remember that God isn't all that far away from us anyway. Jesus told us in John 14:16, "And I will pray to the Father, and He shall give you another Comforter, that He may abide with you for ever" (KJV). We know that this Comforter is the Holy Spirit (see John 14:26) and Jesus said that He will abide with us forever. Here, Comforter is the Greek word *parakletos,* which is another form of *parakaleo*. Therefore, when we cry out to God for His comfort, the Holy Spirit does not have to go very far to help us since He already has taken up residence within us, for we are the temples of the Spirit of God. *Parakletos* actually goes beyond the meaning of comfort; in classical Greek, a *parakletos* was a legal advisor or advocate who came forward on behalf of another to be their representative much like a lawyer today who offers legal representation. However, unlike a lawyer, we don't need to *pay* for Him to come alongside us; we just need to *call out* to Him!

Finally, we need to remember that God comforts us in *all* our afflictions, not just a few, and that *His comfort is continuous and repeated*, as this is what the verb tense that is being used in the Greek means. If we know that God is there through our afflictions, those things that try to *crush, press, or squeeze* us (from the word *thlipsis*), let us receive His healing comfort by choosing to call on the wonderful name of Jesus!

...<u>Now That I Know It, How Do I Live It?</u>...

...comfort

I can't overstate the value and importance of giving comfort to those who are suffering. Even the act of showing comfort to another hurting person—an act as small as a quick hug, an encouraging word, or a squeeze of the hand—can be very healing in and of itself. When we are in pain (emotional, physical or otherwise), it can be so reassuring to receive a gesture or a word of comfort from someone who cares. Scripture instructs us to comfort one another during the difficult times. Even though what we offer to another in the way of comfort may seem small or insignificant to us, it may be just what the person on the receiving end needs to make it through just one more day.

The comfort that the Lord offers us when we're hurting is perhaps one of the most healing experiences that we can have in Him, as He knows how to comfort us perfectly; He knows our deepest needs without our even needing to ask, He knows what we're going through emotionally, and He knows exactly how to minister to us, exactly when we need it. Christ is often depicted in drawings and paintings as holding a sheep in His tender arms of comfort. This picture truly is worth a thousand words, as it is a powerful visual representation of what we can experience when we allow ourselves to be held in His loving grasp. Scripture even tells us in Isaiah 40:11, "In His arms He will gather the lambs and carry them in His bosom." Oftentimes, this is precisely the picture we need of Christ – of Him holding us close to His heart!

The type of comfort He gives is obviously not just physical, but emotional, spiritual, and relational as well. Because Christ Himself was a Man of Sorrows, and because He has walked through and been tempted by all of the same things that we face in our own lives, He *relates* to everything that we go through. Out of His ability to relate with us and our sufferings, He then sends us just the right type of comfort that He knows we need at that moment. We may experience His comfort in a number of different ways, including a peace that washes over us, a strong sense of His presence with us,

His perfect love embedding itself deep within our soul, or an inner knowing that everything will be all right...just to name a few. It grieves Christ when He sees one of His own beloved children hurting or suffering, and His heart goes out to that child to bring the fullness of His healing comfort, as only He can provide.

When we cry out to the Lord, Scripture says that He hears our cry and that *He runs to us*! He runs to us to bring us His comfort; He doesn't just do this once in a while, or from time to time, but *each* time we need Him. We have to trust in the promise of His comfort, and let it minister to our hearts in a way that will not only soothe our wounds and our hurts, but that will bring a full measure of His healing to us as well!

day #8 **peace**

peace

Thou wilt keep him in perfect peace,
whose mind is stayed on thee: because He trusteth in thee.
~ Isaiah 26:3 (KJV) ~

...<u>The Words BEHIND the Word</u>...

When we hear the word peace, what do we often think? Perhaps we think of it as the absence of war, which is how the Greek word for peace, *eirene*, is often used in classical Greek literature. At others times peace may be viewed as tranquility, serenity, or quiet. While these definitions are true, the Bible goes well beyond these meanings of peace.

The Hebrew word for peace is *shalom* and it was used in various ways during the Old Testament period and even continues in its usage today in modern Hebrew as a greeting among people. It comes from the word *shalam* which means *to be whole, safe, uninjured, sound, or peaceful*. Thus, at its root, *shalom* means wholeness. As we look further into this word, we will come to see that this is what God wants for us. This wholeness, or well-being, includes prosperity, health, contentment, peace of mind, and peace in relationships. There are numerous Biblical references to these aspects of peace in the Old Testament. The concept of peace is so important that God desires us to be in "perfect peace." The literal

46

rendering of the text reads *shalom shalom* or "peace peace" and this signifies emphasis in the Hebrew text. Implied here is a peace that is a true, enduring peace, the kind that only God can provide, not merely temporary peace which is what only man can provide. This peace comes from a mind that is steadfast and fixed upon God and trusting in Him. Here, we can find a link to our wholeness, because if we have an unwavering faith and trust in God, we will believe that in spite of our circumstances, God is our Rock and our Fortress, and that His love has not left us. In fact, Phillipians 4:7 tells us that "...the peace of God, which surpasses all comprehension, will guard your hearts and your minds in Christ Jesus." Here, the word "guard" means *to guard with a military guard*, and this is what peace—the perfect peace of God—will do for us.

The concept of peace is culminated in the priestly blessing of Numbers 6:24-26 which states, "The LORD bless you, and keep you; The LORD make His face shine on you, and be gracious to you; the LORD lift up His countenance on you, and give you peace." Peace, therefore, is a gift from God which can only be *received in His Presence!* The blessing is meant to be spoken over an individual so that the person may be blessed, guarded, and treated graciously by God. This depicts a person who is fulfilled and complete—whole—and one who, through the presence of God, has experienced His blessing of peace.

...<u>Now That I Know It, How Do I Live It?</u>...

...*peace*

The verse from a famous hymn describes "peace like a river", and I believe this has much truth to it. Peace has a flowing, calming, and soothing nature about it that is difficult to describe accurately in words. It is that inner knowing that, despite even the most tumultuous of circumstances, we have a strong, immovable and steadfast core of peace residing in our "spirit-man." Scripture says that it "transcends understanding", because it truly does! How in the natural realm would it ever make sense for a man to be filled to overflowing with peace while in prison surrounded by despairing and threatening circumstances? And yet, this is exactly the type of true peace the Lord makes available to each of us; we need only call upon Him and ask Him to provide it for us in our hearts. Peace of this sort has *absolutely nothing* to do with circumstances, and *absolutely everything* to do with standing firm and staying grounded despite our circumstances. It is a way for us to transcend, or "rise above", whatever is happening on earth in our lives, and to allow God to "elevate" us above those circumstances to gain His perspective on them.

It has been said that when faced with a decision—and a desire to make a *wise* decision—one should ask the Lord to be guided either by peace or turmoil. There is merit to this because God is never the author of confusion (turmoil), and His yoke is easy and His burden is light, so when we submit our situation to Him, He will guide our footsteps in such a way as to bring us peace in terms of the direction we are to take. Now certainly He guides through other venues as well, but peace is one way that He can choose to do so.

At the center of peace, there is the absence of struggle. And of striving, and of toiling, overanalyzing, and so forth. Sometimes in our walk with the Lord, we tend to make things much more difficult than they actually need to be, or should be. We can easily work ourselves up into a frenzy over a situation, having consulted with many other believers and sought their opinions, before we finally quiet ourselves long enough to hear the still small voice from within speak to us. The Lord is a gentleman; He will never force Himself or His will on any of us. But He stands and waits patiently while we exhaust ourselves—and our resources—trying to figure out the solution to a problem when all along, we need have only looked upward into His calm and peaceful face, and sought our answer there. "Peace, be still...", our Lord says to us in the times of the storms of our lives (Mark 4:39).

Therefore let us draw near with confidence to the throne of grace, so that we may receive mercy and find grace to help in time of need.
~ Hebrews 4:16 ~

...<u>The Words BEHIND the Word</u>...

The concept of God's grace is central to the Christian faith. It is because of God's grace that we have salvation through faith in Jesus Christ. It is only through God's grace, and not our works, that we can live with Him forever in heaven (see Ephesians 2:8). Once we understand the concept of God's grace, it can bring so much healing into our lives.

The Greek word for grace, *charis*, comes from the verb *chairo* which means *to rejoice, or to be glad*. In addition, the root *char* indicates something which produces well-being. Thus, *charis* means *grace, that which causes joy, pleasure or delight, a kindness granted or desired, gratitude or thanks*. It is a favor done on behalf of another and it is truly an unmerited or undeserved favor. When a repentant sinner receives God's grace and forgiveness through faith in His Son, it brings into that person's life joy and thankfulness to God. This grace transforms us and causes us to love God and to seek His righteousness. Initially, God's grace brings regeneration to our spirits through the work of the Holy Spirit. As we continue in our Christian walk, we need a constant supply of God's grace, and as we remain in the grace of God, it will ensure we will persevere until the end of life. This is the process of sanctification; it is a work of God where we are becoming renewed day by day and are enabled to daily die unto sin and to live our lives unto righteousness.

Since we have been forgiven through the atonement of Christ due to the grace of God, we now have access to the throne of God. Hebrews 4:16 encourages us to approach God's throne with boldness. This boldness is the word *parresia* and it means *freedom in speaking, confidence, openness, or boldness*. As we come to God in an attitude of thanksgiving for His grace, we can bow ourselves before His throne—His throne of grace—and speak openly about the desires of our hearts. We do not need to be in fear, for the gracious work of Christ on the cross has made our access possible. In fact, as we approach God's gracious throne with openness, we will receive mercy, and then find His grace helping us in our time of need. This time of need is a compound of two Greek words meaning *good, eu*, and *a critical moment or point in time, kairos*. It therefore means something that is *well-timed, or the best point in time to take action*. It is at this point that God will provide us with His help. The root word of "to help" is *boetheo* which is from *boe, a cry*, and *theo, to run*, and it means *to run upon hearing a cry, or to give assistance*. Therefore, God doesn't just provide His help, *He runs to help us when He hears our cry!* God's grace has been extended to us in ways that are beyond what we ever imagined. His grace allows us to have access to Him, to approach Him openly, and because of His grace He runs to help us when we cry out to Him at just the right time. Praise God for His amazing grace!

...<u>Now That I Know It, How Do I Live It?</u>...

...grace

The Lord has perfect grace for all of us, at all times. He expresses it perfectly because He is the Author of it; it is part of His wonderful character. Grace is not bound by a justice system of any sort, because if it were, none of us would ever be granted grace. Grace is not about what is deserved, merited, fair, or even just, because its definition is in direct opposition to all of that. Grace is unmerited, underserved, and even "unfair" or "unjust" at times, in terms of how our human minds conceive of it at least. But in God's kingdom, His grace is the result of His pure love, and is not dependent upon anything we might or might not do. Instead, it is completely independent of our own actions, and completely dependent upon His love and mercy.

Grace is a challenge in all human relationships. It is very hard for many of us to understand and concur with the fact that the Lord expects us to show His amazing grace to those of His children that *we* may not feel are deserving of it. Herein lies the challenge, and also one of the hallmarks of Christian maturity. Can we humble ourselves enough to see that others around us need the same grace that we ourselves have needed and begged God for at so many points in our own lives? It forces us to acknowledge our own flaws and weaknesses, doesn't it? And also, this can be an avenue through which we can find it in our hearts to extend that grace to others.

I address the issue of grace frequently in the marital counseling sessions that I do at my practice, because it seems to be a forgotten treasure for many in relationships with their spouse. I encourage couples to use a short phrase with each other: "I grace you." I encourage the use of this phrase frequently, because it is also the forerunner to warding off a spirit of offense, and to make the process of forgiveness happen a little more easily. When a person you love slights you, hurts you, or makes an insensitive remark to you, instead of responding angrily and defensively, try to respond with grace. Yes, your flesh will battle you very strongly when you do this, but view that as a confirmation that you are indeed making the right choice – a choice to walk after the Spirit and *not* after the flesh. As you put this into practice on a consistent basis, you will find that it truly will become an easier process. And as an unexpected bonus, you may even discover that your extending of grace to your loved one will prompt the same in return for you!

day #10 **faith**

faith

Now faith is the substance of things hoped for,
the evidence of things not seen.
~ Hebrews 11:1 (KJV) ~

...The Words BEHIND the Word...

As stated in the introduction, having faith in the Lord Jesus is essential to our healing. For when faith is present within us, we are prepared to receive God's healing power. In fact, where there is a lack of faith, there may also likely be a lack of God's power being displayed. We can see this in Mark 6:5 where, because of the unbelief of those in Jesus' hometown of Nazareth, He "could do no miracle there except that He laid His hands on a few sick people and healed them." The unbelief of the people did not remove Jesus' ability to heal – it only did not permit the release of what was already present. However, we should not always equate the lack of answer to prayer to a lack of faith on our part. Sometimes we can get down on ourselves because we feel we don't have enough faith. It's important to remember that Jesus was present in Nazareth and possessed the ability to heal; the people however, *chose* to not believe in Him even though they knew of His miracles.

The Greek word for faith is *pistis* which has its origin from the word *peitho* meaning *to win over or persuade*. For example, when

54

we put our faith in Christ for salvation, *we have been persuaded* that we are sinners and that believing in Christ's sacrificial death on the cross brings us forgiveness of our sins. Therefore, *pistis* means *conviction, firm persuasion, or faith.*

In Hebrews 11:1, we can see how faith is demonstrated in our lives, for it is the substance (*hupostasis*) of things hoped for, the evidence (*elegchos*) of things not seen. *Hupostasis* comes from the words *hupo*, meaning *under* and *histemi*, which means *to stand.* Thus, it means *something that stands or is in place under, that which is a support or basis, a substance.* Therefore, faith becomes our rock, our support for the hope we have in God. In fact, this hope is a continuous hoping as this is how the Greek text renders the verb. The word *elegchos* means *conviction* and means not only conviction from God regarding sin, but also conviction in a legal sense where the charge against the accused is revealed and acknowledged. Here, this conviction is regarding "things not seen" which is once again a continuous "not seeing." So we can see the weight that faith carries in our lives and how it refuses to rely upon what is seen; rather, it builds up a firm and concrete foundation and continues to hope in the Living God. As the Apostle Paul says in 2 Corinthians 5:7, "For we walk by faith, not by sight."

...<u>Now That I Know It, How Do I Live It?</u>...
...*faith*

Faith can sometimes seem like a difficult concept to grasp or comprehend because it is not necessarily a tangible thing (at least not in the natural realm!) that we can get our arms around. And yet, faith is one of the key components in our relationship with the Lord. Scripture tells us that without faith, it is impossible to please God. How can we please God, then, if we don't even have much of an idea of what faith is in the first place?

As stated previously, faith can be seen as meaning "to win over or persuade." So in a sense, faith may be viewed as a type of strong belief, so strong that it actually persuades us into a particular point of view about something. We are then "won over" to that side, so to speak. Faith in God pleases Him because He knows that even though we can't "see" Him with our earthly eyes, we have still chosen to believe and trust in Him.

We've all heard the phrase, "Take a step of faith." Taking a step of faith implies taking a risk of some sort, and in a sense, this is true. We can say to the Lord that we'll step out in faith, all the while praying that we'll find a solid rock beneath our feet when we do! So therefore, on some occasions, faith *will* feel like risk, but each and every time we choose to have faith, God makes it more than worth our while. Learning to walk by faith and not by sight is really a life-long process for most of us. As we begin to see God as a Faithful God, it will become easier for us to step out in faith. But it is a process of trust and maturity for all of us. A strong faith in God helps us take what we know to be true in our mind and walk it out in our heart, our everyday experiences. Faith can take head knowledge and turn it into heart knowledge, if we activate our will and make the choice to take a step out in faith, even though the risk of doing so may seem a little intimidating at first. But God supplies all of our needs, and this one is no exception. We can ask the Holy Spirit to give us an increased measure of faith, and He will...just be prepared for some "tests" along the way as He grows your faith and levels of experiencing that faith in Him!

Faith can be seen as a pure level of trust, which is not in need of evidence, or of all the facts, or of "logical explanations." It is a choice despite the lack of these, and it is this characteristic that makes it so vital to our Christian walk, because we couldn't go where God wants to take us without seeing our lives through the lens of faith!

day #11 **repentance**

repentance

For the sorrow that is according to the will of God produces a repentance without regret, leading to salvation, but the sorrow of the world produces death.
~ 2 Corinthians 7:10 ~

...The Words BEHIND the Word...

Our entrance into God's kingdom is through the doorway of repentance and faith in Jesus Christ. However, our repentance should not stop there; rather, it should continue as one of the foundational elements of our Christian life whereby we mature with that foundation already laid (see Hebrews 6:1-2). Unfortunately, it becomes all too easy for us to turn to God for forgiveness for our post-conversion sins, which God is willing to forgive, than to also repent of those sins, which is what God ultimately wants us to do. In order to add repentance back into our lives and be able to understand how repentance brings healing, it will help us to look at the Biblical definition of repentance.

The Apostle Paul contrasts two types of sorrow in 2 Corinthians 7:10: sorrow from God, and sorrow from the world. The Greek word for sorrow, *lupe*, means *grief, sorrow, emotional or physical pain* and is used in the expression *kata Theon lupe* which literally means *sorrow down from or according to God*, and in the expression *tou kosmou lupe* which means *sorrow of or from the world*. When we have sorrow that comes down from God, it literally works and labors in us until it works out or produces life-giving repentance. Sorrow from the world, on the other hand, does not have the same affect as it only works and labors in us until it produces death. It's the same process, but very different results. Obviously, anything that leads to death does not promote healing in our lives. So what are the differences between the two types of sorrow? It's really tied up in the Bible's two different Greek words for repentance, *metanoia* (and the verb form *metanoeo*) and *metamelomai*.

Metanoia is used in the passage above and it is rooted in the words *meta* meaning *together with or a change of condition* and *noeo* meaning *to perceive or to think* which comes from the Greek word for the mind, *nous*. Thus, this word literally means *a change in the condition of how one thinks or perceives in one's mind*! It is this changing of the mind that truly defines the repentance that leads to life. *Metamelomai* is derived from the same *meta*; however, it is compounded with *melo*, which carries a meaning of *being concerned*. Therefore, it has a meaning of *regretting what one has done, or changing one's feelings about something*. It represents more of a feeling of remorse, rather than a fundamental shift in how one views what one has done wrong. It brings an old adage to mind: sorry for being caught (rather than sorrow for what one did). This word is used in the expression "felt remorse" in Matthew 27:3 which states, "Then when Judas, who had betrayed Him, saw that He had been condemned, he felt remorse and returned the thirty pieces of silver to the chief priests and elders." Here, Judas regretted what he had done, as expressed by his worldly sorrow, but he didn't truly repent of his wrongdoing which would have been expressed by Godly sorrow. In the end, Judas' worldly sorrow literally led to death as he took his own life. If we, on the other hand, can truly change our mind about the wrong we've done, the healing process can begin as we choose to get back on the path that God has chosen for us.

...Now That I Know It, How Do I Live It?...

...*repentance*

As stated before, the root of the word *repentance* literally means "to change one's mind." This gives us good insight into exactly what happens when we repent of sin; we are saying to the Lord that we are no longer going to go in that direction, and instead we activate our will to change our mind about the sin. When we do this, we take ownership of what we've done, and choose to no longer continue to participate in that sin. This then gives the Lord an opportunity to work in our hearts and help us strengthen our resolve to not go back into a particular sin situation. Repentance is vitally important because it keeps our heart from being hardened, and as such, our conscience seared, to sin. The longer we stay in sin without repenting, the harder the shell around our heart can become, which is a dangerous place to be in because it then becomes much more difficult for us to sense the conviction that the Holy Spirit brings when we go off track into sin. It's so important that we remain "teachable" and sensitive to the Holy Spirit's leading, because it affects so many areas of our lives, including healing.

I believe that the importance of repentance in the healing process is often underestimated. The reality is that sin has the ability to produce much affliction and suffering in our lives, especially if it is left alone and not addressed or repented of. Through unconfessed sin, we can be hindered from fully walking in the Spirit and receiving the healing that God wants for us in our lives. Also, sin that has not been repented of can very quickly and easily open a door to the demonic realm, giving the enemy "legal ground" to operate in our lives in certain areas. Sin of any kind can serve as a major roadblock, directly or indirectly, in our healing process.

One main indication that sin is at the root of an unhealed issue is the presence of guilt surrounding a particular wound. We need to be aware, of course, that there is also a type of "false guilt" that the enemy uses, along with condemnation, but true guilt is a sign that the Holy Spirit may be bringing conviction to an area of our lives. The Lord gently nudges us to repent; He does not harshly shame or condemn us into it (these are the enemy's tactics), and it's crucial that we know and correctly discern the difference. If we seek God on a regular basis and ask Him to search our hearts, He will shed His light and truth on areas where sin may be at the root of an unhealed emotional or spiritual issue. If this is the case, then we know that our first step to healing is to "change our mind"—repent—and no longer choose to remain in that sin. The Lord is always faithful to show us what is operating in our hearts; we need only to be willing to see it for what it is.

day #12 hope

hope

I wait for the LORD, my soul does wait,
and in His word do I hope.
~ Psalm 130:5 ~

...The Words BEHIND the Word...

One of the most distinguishing features of Biblical Christianity (and Judaism) from all other religions in the world is our hope in God. There have been discoveries of prayers from Israel's neighbors during the Old Testament period. In none of those prayers, do the people ever refer to their "gods" as their hope. However, an Israelite who was a follower of the Lord could pray, "For You are my hope; O Lord GOD, you are my confidence from my youth" (Psalm 71:5). God is the object of our hope, and since He is faithful, merciful, loving, and just, our hope can be fully directed and placed in Him.

In Psalm 130:5, the Hebrew word for hope is *yachal* which means *to tarry or wait, to hope or be expectant, or to be patient.* As we can see, hope is linked with waiting and so often this is what God wants us to do—wait. Though we are waiting, we can still wait expectantly and with hope, for the Lord of Hosts will never fail us. In essence, to hope for something is to wait for something because we do not hope for what we already have, rather for what we desire to have. It is so important for us to have a proper perspective of waiting and hoping for what God has in store for us. If we dig into another Hebrew word for hope, we find an even greater treasure. The word for hope in Psalm 71:5 is *tiqvah*, which carries the meaning of *a cord, an expectation, a hope*. Its root is the word *qavah* which means *to bind together by twisting, to expect, to wait, or to hope*. Thus, as we are hoping in the Lord, this hope becomes a cord or a rope, a lifeline, which ties us into our loving Heavenly Father. As we are remaining in hope and expressing our faith in God, we become bound to Him—even twisted together with Him—believing that He is worthy of our hope.

The main New Testament word for hope, *elpis*, is also rich with meaning. Its usage never refers to a vague or fearful hope; rather, it always conveys the expectation of something good. Hope, along with faith and love, form the three fundamental elements of the Christian life (see 1 Corinthians 13:13). While on earth, none of these three can exist without the others for there is no hope without faith in Christ, who loved us before the foundation of the world. The New Testament shows us that this hope is always Christ-centered, does not rely upon works of the flesh, but the grace of God, and is a gift of the Father's grace. One of the most detrimental attitudes that we can have is one expressing a lack of hope. Scripture, in contrast, argues against that type of attitude, as *elpis* is used 54 times demonstrating an adundance of hope. As the Apostle Paul says in Romans 15:13, "Now may the God of hope fill you with all joy and peace in believing, so that you will abound in hope by the power of the Holy Spirit."

...<u>Now That I Know It, How Do I Live It?</u>...

...hope

A well-known Proverb states "Hope deferred makes the heart sick" (Proverbs 13:12, KJV). This is true for all aspects of our being. Physically, we can actually develop bodily symptoms when hope is absent from our lives, including (amongst many others) lethargy, loss of appetite, and sleep disturbances, ranging from insomnia to hypersomnia (sleeping away most of the day.) Spiritually, if we don't maintain our hope in Christ, who *is* our Hope, we can run the risk of shutting down our prayer life, studying Scripture, and communing with God. When hope is lost, we are less likely to want to attend church and worship. All of these elements are vital to our spiritual "health." And emotionally, if we don't have hope, it can be a definite precursor to depression, and in many cases, major clinical depression, which may require professional help.

It needs to be said that hope, in fact, is a choice! There may be times in our lives when we'll feel hopeful without necessarily "trying" to or choosing to, such as a natural response when we get good news or learn of something that will make our lives better or easier. But, more often than not, we will need to *consciously choose* to be hopeful. And depending upon the circumstances, this may not always be the easiest thing to do, but if we do it, it will help us tremendously in getting through the difficult times and struggles that come with life. Choosing hope means embracing the concept that there actually *is* light at the end of the proverbial tunnel. Choosing hope means that we focus ourselves on looking toward that light, and allowing it to encourage us to keep persevering through our trials.

Part of choosing hope involves the concept of the renewing of our mind, as Scripture instructs us to do. Renewing the mind in relation to choosing hope involves filling the mind with Scriptures that talk about hope, as well as choosing to think hopeful thoughts rather than choosing to think negative thoughts such as "I give up; it's hopeless," or "I can't see the light at the end of the tunnel," or "Why bother hoping; it won't happen anyway" and so forth. These negative types of thoughts are so detrimental to our emotional health, and at times can even bring on signs of depression, as stated above, because our thoughts will lead to feelings very easily.

We can see what can happen when hope is lost; now let's address the numerous benefits that are present when we do choose to hope. The benefits of, or advantages to, choosing and remaining hopeful are many. Some of these can include, for example, experiencing less stress in our lives, as a mindset of hope changes our attitude and outlook on our circumstances, which can reduce our stressful moments, along with making us less vulnerable to depression. Scripture says in Psalm 43:5, "Hope in God: for I shall yet praise Him, who is *the health of my countenance*, and my God" (KJV, emphasis added). Our "countenance" refers to our facial expression, and so when we make it a point to hope in God, it may even reflect on our face! Our inward decision, in this case to choose hope, becomes an outward expression. As believers, we also must not forget "The Blessed Hope" (Titus 2:13), which refers to the glorious appearing of Christ when He comes back for us, His church! A perspective like this can be very encouraging to us when we are in trials of many kinds and need an eternal viewpoint to help get us through.

day #13 trust

trust

When I am afraid, I will put my trust in You. In God, whose word I praise, in God I have put my trust; I shall not be afraid. What can mere man do to me?
~ Psalm 56:3-4 ~

...The Words BEHIND the Word...

"Y ou can't trust anyone nowadays", is a statement we some- times hear. While deception and immorality have increased in our culture which offers little for us to trust in, we still should as Christians strive to be trustworthy individuals and be encouraged to know that we can always trust in God. In Psalm 56, David expressed such a confidence and trust in God, that it almost seems inconceivable. When David was feeling fear for his life because of the pursuit of his enemies, *he chose* to put his trust in God – so much so that he no longer felt afraid since he was being pursued by mere men – but he had put his trust in the living God! We need to note that fear will come up in our lives, but as we choose to trust in God that fear will diminish.

It is often said that fear and faith cannot coexist. If we look at one of the Greek words for trust, it is the word *peitho* which means *to win over, to persuade* and it is the root of the Greek word for faith, *pistis*. When we trust someone, we believe in them and are persuaded that they will do what's best for us. We believe and are convinced of their ability and sincerity, and this is exactly what the word *peitho* means – we have faith in that person and trust them. But how does this faith and trust remove our fear?

Let's turn to the Hebrew word for trust, *batach*, which is used in Psalm 56. *Batach* carries with it the idea of *attaching oneself to another,* and it can mean *to trust, to confide in, or to be secure,* and it has a basic meaning of *something that is firm or solid.* It is a word whereby one individual expresses complete confidence in the other. Thus, when we are expressing our trust in God, we are attaching ourselves to Him and if we are attached to Him, His presence will cast out our fear for "perfect love casts out fear" (1 John 4:18). Therefore, in our relationship with God we can choose to trust in God, and then we can surely let our anxieties go and cling to God…because we know that He is in control and that we can be confident in Him. This is what David chose to do as he actively trusted in God until that trust was fully completed (for this is what the Hebrew verb tense used here is telling us). In other words, he continued the act of tying himself to God until he knew the job was finished. Here, David found healing from his fears; healing that he so desperately needed. Let us do the same and in turn, let us be trustworthy examples in an untrusting world.

...Now That I Know It, How Do I Live It?...

...trust

It can be so difficult to trust at times, can't it? The individuals I see in my practice usually cite trust as one of the top issues that has proven to be a continual struggle for them over the years. For many, trust is so easily shattered, and once it's in pieces, it's very difficult to put those pieces back together again; they never seem to fit in quite exactly the same way. Trust is fragile, and because of this, it needs to be treated as such. If someone confides something to a friend, and then that friend "breaks" their trust, the pain and feelings of betrayal can oftentimes seem overwhelming. We have all been in that boat at one time or another in our lives, and how we respond when our trust has been broken is crucial to our emotional health.

For example, some people, when trust has been violated, will close themselves in and make an agreement with themselves along the lines of "I will never allow myself to become close to anyone again." This is a type of "inner vow", or simply a statement of the will that boxes a person in to a particular response pattern. Inner vows are not easily broken. In many cases, this vow is made subconsciously and the person making it may not even realize that they've done so. But the fruit that comes from a vow like this can be seen easily: a person whose trust has been shattered will likely distance themselves or pull back in many of their relationships, they may hold others at "arm's length", they may refuse to take emotional risks for fear of the hurt that could result, or they may even become cynical and sarcastic, an indication that they are harboring anger deep down as well. In essence, the *fortress* of protection they've built around their heart becomes a *prison* from which they cannot escape.

This is why it is so important that we don't become too invested in trying to protect ourselves from any and all pain that life may hold. If we do this, we will build dozens (if not more) of walls around our heart, never being willing to "let anybody in" for fear that they may hurt us. We need instead to trust that God will protect us; He knows what we can handle, and He will never give us more than that. No matter what man has done to us to hurt our trust, the Lord is fully and completely trustworthy. We never need to fear that God will betray or break our trust; He is a perfect God, and it would be an impossibility for Him to do so. Satan works overtime to try to render us afraid of placing our trust in God, but we need to stand firm against his lies and choose instead, even though it may feel scary at first, to give our heart to the Lord and trust every aspect of our lives to Him. As we make the choice to do so, we will see Him prove Himself consistently and completely trustworthy in our lives.

day #14 gratitude
gratitude

Therefore as you have received Christ Jesus the Lord, so walk in Him, having been firmly rooted and now being built up in Him and established in your faith, just as you were instructed, and overflowing with gratitude.
~ Colossians 2:6-7 ~

...The Words BEHIND the Word...

Gratitude. Thanksgiving. In a world that has becoming increasingly more self-centered and where blessings have become more of an expectation, we can see these words are being used less and less frequently. However, as believers we are instructed over and over again to be filled with gratitude and thanksgiving. In fact, Colossians 2:7 says that we should be overflowing with gratitude!

The Greek word for gratitude in the above verse is *eucharistia,* and this word might look familiar to many of us, as our English word eucharist (which is a term for Holy Communion) is taken from *eucharistia.* If we trace back the roots of this word, it is ultimately formed from *eu* meaning *good or well*, and from *charis* meaning *grace*. Thus, it can be looked at as meaning *good grace or well favored* and it is defined as our response to this good grace by meaning *thanksgiving, gratitude, or thankfulness*. Therefore, gratitude becomes our response to a feeling of being well favored and it becomes quite clear as to why Scripture admonishes us to approach

God with thanksgiving. Since God reached out to us in order to provide an atonement for our sins, we have every reason to feel well favored! So much so that it flows out excessively, with more than enough, around, over and above, as this is what the word *perisseuo*, translated "overflowing", means. If we can adopt this attitude towards the things of God, we can then begin to apply it towards those "little blessings" in our lives. In fact, "every perfect gift is from above" (James 1:17) and as we realize this, it will become easier for us to convey a sense of gratitude.

Scripture also instructs us to be grateful even when we are going through troubles and afflictions or when we are worried or anxious. In Phillipians 4:7, Scripture instructs us to "Be anxious for nothing, but in everything by prayer and supplication with thanksgiving let your requests be made known to God." Here, thanksgiving is translated from the word *eucharistia* and it is to accompany our prayers to God about that which we are anxious. How can we be thankful during these times? If we look at the word for anxiety, *merimnao*, it is derived from the word *meris* which means *a part or portion*. Our anxieties are only a portion of the whole picture! God sees the whole picture and this is surely something for which we can express gratitude to God in our prayers. For when we do, "the peace of God, which surpasses all comprehension, will guard your hearts and your minds in Christ Jesus."

...<u>Now That I Know It, How Do I Live It?</u>...

...gratitude

An attitude of gratitude can literally make or break a person's outlook or perspective on life. Gratitude is so important, in fact, that failure to take note of all of the areas in our lives that deserve our gratitude can actually cause a person to fall into some level of depression! Especially in our Western society today, where we seem to have all of the creature comforts possibly needed, we easily take for granted the many blessings the Lord has bestowed upon our lives. Some of us as human beings seem to be "hardwired" to notice the negatives, to look for and point out those situations or conditions that we are *un*happy with, and some even make sure that everyone around them is aware of their opinions and attitudes as well. It's so easy to fall into a trap like this, and it actually takes discipline to turn an ungrateful heart around!

One thing that I frequently request of the clients I see at my private practice is to ask them to make a list every day of at least 10 things they are grateful for, as part of their prayer time with the Lord each morning. The Bible tells us that God's mercies are new every morning, so we know that in God's creation alone we can find untold riches, beauty, and blessings because of His loving, providential hand towards us, His creation. Surprisingly though, many people struggle greatly with compiling such a list. If that's the case, I will encourage the clients I see to begin by looking at the most basic, fundamental elements, such as the fact that they have "air to breathe" for yet another day. And it truly is okay if it takes time to really incorporate this as a way of thinking, because, in essence, by doing so we are actively engaging in the process that the Bible calls "the renewing of the mind." As we *choose* what we want to fill our thoughts with (in this case, those things which we are grateful for and appreciative of in our lives), and dwell on these thoughts, we will find that we'll soon begin to feel better about ourselves and adopt a more positive attitude about life in general.

If we *choose* to adopt an attitude of gratitude for the blessings we've received, we may then desire to be a blessing to others as well. But if we choose to take the blessings God has put into our lives for granted, we will live with a mentality that says we are entitled to more, deserve better, and as such, we will waste time and energy wondering why "life isn't fair." Gratitude truly is a choice. Even though we may feel that we have very little to be grateful for, we need to start off small with those things we typically skip over because they may seem too inconsequential on the surface.

As you may be aware, the second half of this book is a journal, and I encourage you to turn to the pages designated for "Gratitude", and ask the Holy Spirit to help bring to your mind the blessings with which He has so lovingly graced you. You will be amazed at the positive change in your mood—and in how you see yourself—if you make a practice of pointing out 10 things per day that you are grateful for!

wisdom
wisdom

The fear of the LORD is the beginning of wisdom, and the knowledge of the Holy One is understanding.
~ Proverbs 9:10 ~

...<u>The Words BEHIND the Word</u>...

In order to begin exercising wisdom in our lives, we need to know where wisdom comes from. The book of Proverbs makes it clear that the "fear of the LORD is the beginning of wisdom" and since Proverbs 2:6 says "the LORD gives wisdom", this makes it quite clear that God is the author of wisdom, and our reverential fear of Him will lead us to greater and greater wisdom.

The Hebrew word for wisdom is *chokmah,* and it is derived from the word *chakam,* meaning *to act wise, be intelligent, to be clever.* It is important to note that in the Jewish mind, wisdom was not just philosophical, but generally very practical because it came from a personal God and pertained to what He revealed about right and wrong, and how that applied to everyday life. Therefore, this wisdom went beyond head knowledge and went more deeply into the aspect of heart knowledge. Also included in the Jewish concept of wisdom were knowledge, experience, insight, and even the ability to perform an occupation.

The best way to see how wisdom promotes healing in our lives is to look at how the exercising of wisdom will keep us from those things that may cause us pain. In the New Testament, the Greek word for wisdom is *sophia* and one of its usages is in James 3:17, where James says, "But the wisdom from above is first pure, then peaceable, gentle, reasonable, full of mercy and good fruits, unwavering, without hypocrisy." These are the fruits of wisdom and they are a tell-tale sign that we are operating in the wisdom that comes from God. It is important to note that the attributes of wisdom listed here are not just intellectual understanding; rather, they are knowing how to act in the appropriate situations. In contrast to this is the wisdom that comes from the world, our own nature, or from the demonic, and it is manifested as bitter envying, strife or selfish ambition, and even arrogance. The result of operating in this type of wisdom "is disorder and every evil thing" (James 3:16). The word for "disorder" is *akatastasia* which is a compound of *a* meaning *not*, *kata* meaning *down*, and *histemi* meaning *to stand,* and thus it literally means *not standing or settled down in its place, unsettled or unstable*. If we want stability in our lives, then we surely want to make certain that we are adhering and listening to God's wisdom and exercising that wisdom throughout our daily lives.

...Now That I Know It, How Do I Live It?...

...wisdom

Possessing true wisdom is one of the most valuable aspects of our walk with and our maturity in the Lord. Without it, we can so easily make poor choices, be drawn astray into deception, form covenant relationships with people we shouldn't, squander our money...the list, quite obviously, is endless! The wisdom that we exercise in our lives is similar to the rudder that steers a ship; each time we make a wise choice, no matter how small or insignificant it may seem at the time, our "ship" continues to move forward on the right path that the Lord has pre-ordained for us. And God's path is always best for us, because He planned it out before any of us were even conceived. When we don't exercise wisdom, however, even if we just veer a little bit off course, we will always need to come back to using God's wisdom in order to set our ship going in the right direction once again. No one does this perfectly all the time! It is most certainly a continual, lifelong process of trial and error, but the Lord will reward us if we persist in traveling according to His will and wisdom for our lives.

Scripture tells us that God's people (us!) *perish for lack of knowledge*. This means that there are so many poor choices that we could easily *avoid* if only we would spend more time in God's presence—getting to know Him; and also spend more time in the Bible—getting to know His Word. God's wisdom is already available to us, just for the asking! We don't have to struggle to get it or strive to figure it out; the Lord *wants* us to walk according to His wisdom, because He knows that we will perish without it! The very cry of our heart can be that God give us His wisdom in all areas of our lives. He will show us the way, and in many ways He has already shown us the way; it is all recorded in His word, with one particular book being known in particular for its immense impartation of words of wisdom—Proverbs. If any of us ever feels that we are lacking in wisdom, Proverbs is a great place to begin. It will keep us, in many ways, from the dangerous condition of ignorance. It offers us the best possible advice for life's situations—God's advice! And if we will heed His words and wisdom, we can spare ourselves from so much pain which can often result when we don't incorporate His wisdom into our lives. When we don't seek God's wisdom, we can also rob ourselves from the healing that He has in store for our lives, because we don't bother to learn all we can from His word about our current state or situation, which leaves us open to some of the enemy's "counterfeit" remedies for healing, instead of God's healing truth. Just to give one example, some people (both believers and non-believers) ignorantly seek healing through New Age methods—which are counterfeits that the realm of darkness has set up to deceive us. It's not that these people are purposely trying to be disobedient to God, but it is because of their lack of wisdom and knowledge on what these methods really are! So it is vitally important that we stay informed enough, and have adequate wisdom and knowledge, to avoid being pulled into a deceptive situation like this.

One simple way to start to make seeking God's wisdom a priority in life is to read one chapter from Proverbs on a daily basis. And then once we've read and meditated on each Proverb and what it means, we can take our *head knowledge* of it and "move it down 18 inches", into our heart, to make it *heart knowledge*. Only when we live out God's word in our heart will it transform our lives!

obedience

obedience

Has the LORD as much delight in burnt offerings and sacrifices as in obeying the voice of the LORD? Behold, to obey is better than sacrifice, and to heed than the fat of rams.
~ 1 Samuel 15:22 ~

...The Words BEHIND the Word...

O bedience is not a very popular concept nowadays. In general terms, obedience requires an acknowledgement of, and a submission to, an authority. The highest form of obedience is our submission to God. Jesus Christ portrayed perfect obedience, as He only did and said what His Father had commanded Him (see John 12) and was obedient even unto death on the cross (Phillipians 2:8). Let's take a look further into the Hebrew and Greek words for obedience.

In 1 Samuel 15:22, the word *shama* is translated "to obey" and it means *to hear, to listen, to obey*, while the word "heed" is taken from *qashav*, meaning *to prick up (as in the ears), to listen, to pay attention*. Therefore, we can see that one of the fundamental meanings of obedience is to hear. If we are respecting the one who is speaking to us, this is the first step to our obedience, as we will then be receptive to hear. This hearing and pricking the ears is so important to God that Samuel told King Saul it would have been better for him to obey what Samuel had told him to do, rather than offering

78

sacrifices, since obedience to God is one of our highest forms of worship. God takes obedience so seriously that in verse 23, He says through Samuel, "For rebellion is as the sin of divination, and insubordination is as iniquity and idolatry." Here, rebellion is equated to divination which is a form of witchcraft! God takes our obedience seriously! In the Old Testament, continual disobedience on the part of the nation of Israel resulted in God's judgment and their eventual exile from the land.

Turning now to the New Testament, the word for obedience is *hupakoe* which is taken from the words *hupo* meaning *under* and *akouo* meaning *to hear*. Thus it literally means *to hear under*, so we can see how this becomes obedience because one is "hearing under the authority of another", which results in obedience. Therefore, one has literally placed themselves under another who is in authority. This is contrasted with the word for disobedience, *parakoe*, which is from the word *para* meaning *along side or to the side of* and *akouo*. The literal meaning here is *to hear to the side of* and it depicts one who lets the voice of another fall to the ground. In fact, it sounds much like the phrase "falling on deaf ears", and it seems to indicate one who moves out from under another's authority. Having God as our ultimate authority does not take the fun out of our lives or become something that is burdensome. Being able to do what we want is not freedom; instead, sin is what leads us into bondage, not obedience. Quite the contrary, obedience actually results in our lives becoming freer. If we look at Deuteronomy 28, we can see that God has set forth blessings for obedience and curses for disobedience, with some of them relating to our physical and emotional health. God really encourages us to place ourselves under His authority, to hear Him, and to obey Him, as this is part of our path to healing and wholeness!

...Now That I Know It, How Do I Live It?...

...*obedience*

Embedded in the word "obedience" is the word "die." Dying to self is one of the key components of obedience, as it is often-times our own desires of our flesh that can lead us directly into disobedience to God's best for us. Obedience—and disobedience—are acts of the will, meaning that we need to purpose in our hearts that we will obey, regardless of how we may feel at the moment. If we wait until we feel like obeying, we will be waiting for a day that never comes! Obedience is a *decision*, despite how we feel. As we align our will with God's and choose to obey Him, our feelings will follow; they may not follow right away, but as we stand firm in our decision to obey, eventually our emotions will catch up.

Believe it or not, there is tremendous potential for healing in being obedient to God! This is due in large part to the fact that we can spare ourselves a lot of unnecessary pain by choosing the path of obedience, rather than operating outside of God's will and feeding our own desires of the moment. We make things so much harder for ourselves when we disobey; God wants to spare us from needless hurt and difficulties by offering us the opportunity to obey Him and walk according to His purposes. But if we continue to repeatedly *dis*obey, we run the risk of hardening our hearts and searing our conscience, making it harder to hear God's still, small voice. This can land us in a very dangerous place both emotionally and spiritually, because when we can't hear His voice of correction and direction, we will find it easier and easier to remain in a state of disobedience, and even rationalize it so that it no longer seems like a significant issue. At this point, we also become an easy target for the enemy, as he now has legal ground to bring harass-ment and torment.

The good news is that the moment we choose to repent and follow the path of obedience again, the Lord empowers us by His supernatural strength to begin to walk according to His plan for us. When we activate our will and tell Him that we are done trying to do things our own way, He meets us where we are and gives us exactly what we need to get back on track. Healing begins to occur on many levels when we align ourselves into obedience to God; our heart softens, our ability to hear Him sharpens, our desire to stay yielded to Him brings a strong and lasting peace to our soul and spirit, and our joy returns as well! A well-known hymn professes: "Trust and obey, for there's no other way to be happy in Jesus, than to trust and obey." If we continually and consistently make the decision to obey Him, we can know true and lasting happiness!

day #17 mercy

mercy

It is of the LORD's mercies that we are not consumed,
because His compassions fail not.
They are new every morning: great is thy faithfulness.
~ Lamentations 3:22-23 (KJV) ~

…The Words BEHIND the Word…

If grace could be interpreted as giving us what we don't deserve, then mercy can be interpreted as not giving us what we do deserve. We can see this so clearly in God's redeeming plan for mankind, as all of us have sinned and deserve God's judgment, yet through God's grace and our belief in the atonement of Christ, *God does not give us what we do deserve.* If God had not reached out to us out of His own love, we could say with the Apostle Paul, "we are of all men most miserable" (1 Corinthians 15:19, KJV).

Mercy is a core attribute of God's character, since when He revealed himself to Moses in Exodus 34:6, He proclaimed "The LORD, the LORD God, merciful and gracious, longsuffering, and abundant in goodness and truth." The Hebrew word for mercy is *chesed* and it means *mercy or lovingkindness.* It is best defined as love or kindness that is displayed in the form of action from one person to another. This display of kindness is usually done in the context of close friends or family members and as such it is based upon the existence of a relationship. However, it does not have to stop here, as mercy can be shown to a stranger. Here, the one displaying the mercy has chosen to treat the other as if the relationship did exist. *Chesed* also carries with it a meaning that is closely tied to a covenant relationship. This meaning conveys the bonds of the covenant relationship whereby each partner owes the other. It is out of God's covenant relationship with His people that His mercy is expressed, as He has chosen to continue His relationship with us even if we do not always remain faithful to Him. Therefore, we can see wrapped up in the definition of mercy is love, strength, and steadfastness, as *chesed* is an act of mercy that is born out of love, and continues to remain steadfast in strength towards another in spite of the other's response. It is this *chesed* of God that we so desperately need and which can bring such an overflow of love to our hearts as we begin to grasp how wonderful and merciful our heavenly Father is toward us.

The New Testament word for mercy, *eleos*, carries with it a similar meaning as *chesed* and is defined as *mercy, compassion, or pity*. It too is an action that is displayed from one individual to another. One of the means whereby we receive mercy is by showing mercy to others. Jesus said in Matthew 5:7, "Blessed are the merciful, for they shall receive mercy." The word translated "blessed" is *makarios* and it means *blessed, having the favor of God*. This type of blessing is a fulfillment that is in God rather than in circumstances that are favorable. As we walk in God's mercy, and show that mercy to others, we will reap the healing rewards of mercy in our own lives.

...Now That I Know It, How Do I Live It?...

...mercy

A practical definition for the concept of mercy could be "compassion in action"; mercy can be viewed as the demonstrative component of compassion, because when we have mercy on or show mercy to another person, we are acting out of the compassion that we feel towards him or her in our heart. An act of mercy toward someone can be a very healing gift; it might even be considered a form of unconditional love, in that we are choosing to show mercy to a person when perhaps it is the last thing they truly "deserve." We hear about people who have a "mercy gift"; these people are usually moved to impart the true *gift* of mercy upon another, and it has become part of their character to do so. Imagine the changes that would occur in our world if more of us operated in showing mercy toward others!

God's word says that His mercies toward us are "new every morning." This is an amazing concept that more of us need to grasp. We can count on the fact that each and every day, there are numerous ways that the Lord is showing mercy toward us, acting out of the compassion that He has on each one of us as His children. As we reflect upon this concept of God's mercy, it can aid in our mind renewal process since we'll begin to view each day as a day whereby God will provide us with sufficient mercy. So if we wake up in the morning feeling a little under the weather, or are experiencing some level of depression or oppression regarding the events of the previous day, we can thank God that *He was* merciful to us yesterday, that *He is* merciful to us this day, and that *He will be* merciful to us tomorrow as well!

To be on the receiving end of God's mercy is a truly humbling experience, because we have the knowledge that our actions deserve some kind of consequence or ramification, and yet God is acting from a standpoint of true mercy upon us. When we are shown mercy, whether by God or by another person, it serves as a reminder to us of our fallen humanity and the fact that we do indeed fail at times, even though our desire is to be pleasing to God. It keeps us aware of the truth that our spirit is willing, but our flesh is weak…yet even so, our God is merciful! The gratitude that we feel from receiving God's mercy can be just the motivation that we need to begin to show mercy on another person. When we pass mercy along to others because we've received mercy from the Lord, mercy becomes a kind of "contagious" action that gains momentum and strength as more people choose to exercise it in the lives of those around them.

Mercy comes full circle in this sense, and it can be a very healing component in our relationships with others. Mercy is foundational to the restoration of broken or damaged relationships, and it models the unconditional love that Christ has toward us. When we extend mercy to someone who has hurt us, it elicits a response in their heart, and so a softening occurs in both directions, which can lay the groundwork for reconciliation. Showing mercy to someone who has brought us pain is most certainly not an easy step to take, and it requires a level of spiritual maturity, but if we're willing to do so, we will also experience a blessing in our own lives because we are following through with what the Lord is asking of us.

day #18 joy

joy

. . . Weeping may endure for a night, but joy cometh
in the morning.
~ Psalm 30:5 (KJV) ~

…The Words BEHIND the Word…

Often times we might hear the word joy and ascribe the attributes of happiness to joy. However, it is so important for us to understand that happiness depends upon our circumstances while true joy does not. Joy was so evident in the early Christian church as it is seen to be woven throughout the New Testament. Having joy in the Lord is not something of a bygone Christian era—it is something that we can still experience today.

There are a number of Hebrew words for joy and *rinnah*, which is used in Psalm 30:5, is one example. It comes from the word *ranan* which means *to shout (usually for joy), to rejoice, to sing.* So we can see that *rinnah* is a type of joy that is vocal and expresses itself. It is a joy that cannot be expressed by mere words alone, rather it brings about a shout of gladness or a song of rejoicing. In Psalm 30:5, joy is contrasted with weeping or *bekee* which is derived from *bakah* meaning *to weep, wail, or bemoan.* This weeping and wailing endures, it temporarily lodges and stays, for the evening, but in the morning there are great shouts of joy for when the weeping breaks and the joy comes, we cannot help but to shout to God in praise. Just as a sparrow finds her nest in the night since the day has been spent, a shout of joyful singing comes again in the morning for the new day has come. We, too, can be encouraged that the time of affliction will be followed by a time of joyful singing.

The New Testament word for "joy" is *chara* while "to rejoice" is *chairo*, from which the word for grace is derived. There is such a strong connection between joy and grace. When a sinner repents and experiences the saving grace of God, the angels in heaven rejoice (Luke 15:10). Once we have received salvation, we experience true and lasting joy for Jesus said in John 16:22, "Therefore you too have grief now; but I will see you again, and your heart will rejoice, and no one will take your joy away from you." Here again we see a time of sorrow followed by a time of rejoicing. One of the most amazing occurrences in the New Testament is the presence of joy in the apostles in spite of the persecution they were enduring. In fact, the apostles actually *rejoiced* that they suffered shame for the name of Christ (Acts 5:41)! How could they do this? How could Paul rejoice while in prison? When they were in tribulations and afflictions (*thlipsis* from the word *thlibo* meaning *to press, crush, or squeeze*) they were able to base their joy in the hope and confidence of faith in the Lord, not in their circumstances. They realized that there are tribulations in this world; however, there awaited for them, and for us, a heavenly home where tears and pain and crying shall all be swept away.

...<u>Now That I Know It, How Do I Live It?</u>...

...joy

A question I hear a lot at my counseling practice is, "What is the difference between joy and happiness?" There are many different opinions on the answer to that question, and as for my own take on it, I tend to view happiness as more *dependent upon* circumstances in life, whereas I view joy as *independent* of the circumstances in life. In other words, I believe it is relatively easy for a person to feel a sense of happiness when some things have gone right in their life; for example, getting accepted into a college he or she had applied to, finding a new friend with whom they realize they share a lot of common interests, inheriting a substantial amount of money to pay down a mortgage, and so forth. (And it must be said here as well that just because any of the above-mentioned situations occur, that is no guarantee for happiness either!) But joy, on the contrary, seems to refer more to a spiritual condition between us and the Lord that maintains stability *despite* the changing circumstances of life.

Joy, believe it or not, can also be practiced in a sense. For example, when a piece of bad news crosses our path, we can choose to rejoice anyhow, verbally proclaiming to the Lord that we are going to choose joy (and even "consider it pure joy", as Scripture instructs) despite the troubling situation that just arose. To take it a step even beyond that, we can choose to rejoice, sing praises, and worship God right at that moment so that our frame of mind lines up with His and the perspective that He would want us to have when faced with any challenge, because nothing is too difficult for Him. Worship has been touted as one of the most effective forms of spiritual warfare as well, partly due to the fact that satan himself cannot stand to be in the presence of believers worshipping God. Scripture tells us to "call those things that aren't as though they were", which leads in to why I believe it's helpful to proclaim God's praises out loud. We learn by hearing, even when it's just hearing our own voice dropping back down into our spirit. So as we make statements aloud such as, "Lord, I choose to experience your joy right now and to rejoice in you even though I don't see the outcome yet" can work wonders for building up your spirit and encouraging your heart. It may seem counterintuitive at first to give joy to God for something that is making us suffer or causing us hardship, but God is known to operate in "counterintuitive ways" at times...Try it for yourself, and evaluate how you feel after you've brought Him a "sacrifice of praise" by giving Him joy in times of difficulty.

day #19 worship
worship

Give unto the LORD the glory due unto His name; worship the LORD in the beauty of holiness.
~ Psalm 29:2 ~

…The Words BEHIND the Word…

We were created to worship God, and God made the desire to worship part of the very fabric of our being – but the choice is ours whether we choose to worship God or to worship something else. God is not the only one who desires our worship – satan has been seeking worship since his rebellion and his desire to ascend to the throne of God. Worship was the goal satan had in mind when he tempted Jesus by offering to hand over to Him the kingdoms of this world. Jesus' response was, "You shall worship the Lord your God, and serve Him only" (Matthew 4:10). We can see, therefore, that our lives are in the midst of a constant battle of whom or what we will worship, and to whom or to what we will bow down.

The Hebrew word for worship is *shachah* and its basic meaning is *to depress*. This "depression" generally refers to the position or posture of our physical bodies, as *shachah* means *to bow down, to prostrate, to fall down, or to worship*. Though a person would not always physically prostrate themselves, other times they would fall upon their knees and touch their forehead to the ground, indicating their full submission to the one to whom they are bowing down or worshipping. Sometimes for us, it is actually healing to bow before the Lord in such a manner because in essence, we are acknowledging that He is God and Lord, and that we are not. We are giving Him the glory due His name and are not trying to take that glory for our own. It's not that God wants to see us groveling in the mud so that He can come and place His foot on our necks showing His power over us; rather, He wants us to willingly submit to Him out of love and reverence for Him since He knows that a humble servant is an obedient servant. It is from this place of worship that God can begin to accomplish His plans through our lives. As long as we continue to bow before something else, it will have control over our lives, and it will never bring us the healing that we need.

This type of bowing down is sometimes associated with the New Testament word for worship, *proskuneo*, which is from *pros*, meaning *towards*, and *kuneo*, meaning *to kiss*. Thus, it means *to kiss towards someone, to show respect, to lay prostrate before, or to worship.* In the ancient Persian world, those of equal rank would kiss each other on the lips, those of slightly different rank would kiss each other on the cheek, while those whose rank was much different, the lower ranking individual would fall upon their knees and touch their forehead to the ground while throwing kisses to the superior. If we express our love towards God in this manner, by laying before Him and throwing kisses toward Him, we will begin to experience His presence in a deeper and more meaningful way.

...<u>Now That I Know It, How Do I Live It?</u>...

...worship

Worship can be a vital key to our healing, though it may not seem like an obvious component at first. But there are several reasons why it is so important. First of all, we were *created* to worship God, and if we don't worship Him, we will end up worshipping something—or someone—else. It has been said that we all have a God-shaped vacuum within that only He can fill. When we choose not to fill it with God, we run the risk of becoming addicted to whatever we choose to fill it with: anything and everything from alcohol, drugs, sex, and material wealth...to relationships or to another person. We can create an idol out of virtually anything, and this is an area where satan will try to get us distracted by and enslaved to everything *but* God, because then we will never find the one and only thing that can bring true and lasting satisfaction. Man's need to worship God is as strong as the enemy's attempts to prevent us from doing exactly that.

In addition, when we worship God, Scripture says that we literally enter into His presence. And when we are in His presence, we are *transformed*. This happens on a spiritual level, the healing effects of which can reach into all aspects of our being: emotional, psychological, and even physical. When we are in God's presence, our focus is solely on Him, and because of this, our perspective on our current struggles in life can change. We can begin to see situations from a vantage point closer to God's perspective rather than our own, which can encourage and edify our hearts, and also bring us a renewed sense of hope. As such, I believe that worship can also help to lift a depression or an oppression, in part because of the change of focus and perspective, and also because of what the Lord can do for us supernaturally when we are in His presence. Even listening to praise music when we are having a difficult or draining day can contribute to lifting our mood; studies done on this phenomenon report fascinating results.

Also, worship is a very effective form of spiritual warfare. The enemy hates it when we worship God, and I believe that he flees from us when we do so. Because worship is what Lucifer sought for himself in the beginning, and which was the cause for his rebellion and his being cast out of Heaven, the last place he wants to be is in the presence of a believer who is praising and exalting God. As such, worship can be seen as a spiritual warfare weapon of choice that can help us tremendously when we sense that we're under demonic attack, as attacks can oftentimes be a major roadblock in our healing process.

day #20 holiness

holiness

As obedient children, do not be conformed to the former lusts which were yours in your ignorance, but like the Holy One who called you, be holy yourselves also in all your behavior; because it is written, "YOU SHALL BE HOLY, FOR I AM HOLY."
~ 1 Peter 1:14-16 ~

…The Words BEHIND the Word…

For the life of the believer, holiness really isn't an option – it is the kind of life that God wants us to live. And no, it is not some pie-in-the-sky perfection or some greater-than-thou attitude in our hearts; rather, it is quite simply being set apart for God and acting in accordance with the new nature that He has given us, instead of acting in accordance with our old nature.

The word for holiness is *hagiosune*, derived from the word for holy, *hagios*, which has the additional meanings of *set apart, consecrated, sanctified, or saint*. At its root, it means *separation*. Thus, to truly be holy is to be separated or set apart; this is the same word that is used to describe the Holy Spirit. The Hebrew word for holy, *qodesh*, carries with it a similar meaning such as *sacredness, apartness, separateness, or holiness*. It is rooted in the word *qadash* which means *to be clean,* and therefore implies "that which is clean is set apart from that which is not." God, who is pure and without sin, is set apart from His fallen creation because of the sin of man.

However, through an act of His grace, God has restored us to fellow-ship with Him and now calls us saints, or the holy ones, which also comes from the word *hagios*. In fact, according the Ephesians 1:4, "He chose us in Him before the foundation of the world, that we would be holy and blameless before Him." It is God's will that we would be holy and He planned that for us even before the world began. The Apostle Paul also exhorts us in 2 Corinthians 7:1 whereby he says, "Therefore, having these promises, beloved, let us cleanse ourselves from all defilement of flesh and spirit, perfecting holiness in the fear of God." The promises that he is referring to are God's statement of walking among and dwelling in His people as He is calling His people to be separate.

It is quite clear from the above passages that God makes us holy, He declares us holy, but He also wants us to live out our lives as holy. This is the process known as working out our salvation (Phillipians 2:12), where we learn to say no to sin, the flesh, and the devil, and learn to say yes to God. Through this process, also commonly referred to as the "sanctification process", we need to remember that sin leads to death and that living a life of abstinence from sin, a holy life that is set apart from this world, brings us into the fuller life that God desires, because He knows that choosing to be holy will benefit us, whereas sin will harm us. One of the highest forms of worship that we can give God is our choosing to be like Him – holy and set apart from sin.

...<u>Now That I Know It, How Do I Live It?</u>...

...holiness

The word *holy*, at its core, carries the meaning of being "set apart." When we have a true desire to be set apart—to be holy—for the Lord, it can be one of the most healing opportunities for us, both emotionally and spiritually. When we choose to sanctify ourselves and our lives unto God for His purposes in us, it makes it that much easier to get "untangled" from all of the things of this world which keep us wrapped, bound, and tied down. We don't need to stay in bondage to anything that the world offers, because our identity in Christ tells us that we are holy...set apart. When we choose to come into right agreement with who God says we are, we can release ourselves from those things that keep us tied to the world. What an awesome freedom to know that we have a choice as to whether or not to remain bound!

If we will choose to walk out our holiness—to decide that we will live our lives as being truly set apart for Him—we will know tremendous blessing from the Lord. He will provide us with the strength that we will need to be *in* this world, but not *of* it. The Lord also knows that there is a price that we will pay for walking out lives of holiness. We will certainly feel a sense of separateness from all that is going on around us in the world; we may feel that we are more like a sojourner in this world rather that a permanent member of it; we may face rejection, ridicule, and isolation at times because of our decision to live according to how the Lord desires us to live, instead of according to how the world desires us to live. But the reward will be like none another—to have the constant knowledge that we are living our lives as pleasing to our King, and walking according to our true identity of being "set apart" for Him—will more than recompense us for the transient difficulties we may face in the process.

We can make this whole process either easier on ourselves or more difficult, depending upon how invested we are in our commitment to remain set apart for Christ. If we have a rock-solid commitment to stay on the path He has for us (and yes, we'll still face many temptations to lean in the direction of the world), our heart will bring us back to our priority of walking in holiness. But if we waver at all, if we tend to swing back and forth quite frequently between wanting to remain separate for God but also wanting to see what the world can offer us, we will be walking a fence that may not be sturdy enough to hold us. If we're divided in our loyalties, we run a major risk for becoming doubleminded, and there really is no more miserable place to be emotionally and spiritually than to be constantly unstable and wavering between two opinions. This will inevitably take its toll on us, and will affect all areas of our lives if we don't make an effort to stay obedient to our God and live a life of holiness, through His strength!

day #21 confession

confession

If we confess our sins, He is faithful and righteous to forgive us our sins and to cleanse us from all unrighteousness.
~ 1 John 1:9 ~

…The Words BEHIND the Word…

"Come on, it's time to 'fess up'!" Most of us have probably heard one of our parents say that to us when we were children. Realizing we were caught, we likely "spilled the beans" and admitted to our wrongdoing and then awaited the punishment that was soon to come. Sadly, for some of us, this punishment may have crossed the line into abuse; however, the mere act of confessing our sins does promote spiritual, emotional, and sometimes even physical healing and as such, should be looked at in a positive and not a negative light.

The Greek word for "confess" in 1 John 1:9 is *homologeo,* and it is formed from the words *homos* meaning *the same,* and *lego* meaning *to say.* Many of us will probably recognize "homo" as it is used in words like "homonym" which means "to sound the same, but have a different meaning." Thus, *homologeo* means *to speak the same thing, to agree with, to confess or profess.* When we became Christians, we confessed with our mouths that Jesus is Lord (see Romans 10:9). In essence what we were doing was agreeing with what was already true – God the Father through the power of the

Holy Spirit raised Jesus the Son from the dead and pronounced Him Lord. Therefore, we spoke the same word as what God had already said—"Jesus is Lord"—and this led to the healing of our spirits. Otherwise, if we didn't agree with what God was saying, we would eventually end up in the lake of fire for eternity, separated from Him. The choice is ours.

Once we become Christians, our confession doesn't stop. We'll continue to sin and we need to continue to confess out our sin to God – not for salvation but for restoration of our relationship with Him. Sin always places a barrier between us and God, and us and others if we sin against other people. Confession is one way to start breaking down these barriers and restoring our relationships. What else happens when we don't confess? Let's take a look at what happened to David in Psalm 32 to find out. In verse 1, he states the benefits of God's forgiveness, for he says, "How blessed is he whose transgression is forgiven, whose sin is covered." The reason David could state this is because he knew what it was like to experience the opposite which is evident in verses 3 and 4: "When I kept silent about my sin, my body wasted away through my groaning all day long. For day and night Your hand was heavy upon me; my vitality was drained away as with the fever heat of summer." When David failed to confess his sin, he experienced both *emotional and physical pain*! Now, God will never *force* us to confess, but He can sure make it difficult for us not to! What is God's goal here? It is not that He wants us to suffer in turmoil, but He wants us to admit what He already knows so that He can bring His healing. Sometimes there still may be consequences to our sin, but there is nothing like having a restored relationship with God. Above all, we need to remember we'll never find healing in sin or covering it up – we will only find healing by exposing sin to the light, and by obeying God and His word. So when we do sin, let's get in the habit of confessing it...*speaking the same word!* After all, He already knows it anyway!

...<u>Now That I Know It, How Do I Live It?</u>...

...*confession*

As we have seen above, the Greek word for *confession* literally means to *speak the same word* as what God already knows to be true about you. In this sense, it is fairly easy to see why speaking out of our mouth those things that we know to be operating in us, or wearing us down, or in need of healing, is the first main step in engaging ourselves in the actual process of allowing the Lord to bring His healing power into our hearts and into our lives. Verbally speaking these issues aloud is a vitally important component of emotional healing. You may wonder why they need to be spoken out loud. I believe that, for one, when something that's been affecting you in your heart is finally outwardly verbalized, it becomes real and reinforces the reality of that situation. Another reason for confessing aloud is that once we get something out in the open, satan no longer has as much power to use that thing against us anymore to inwardly bring torment. Once we've exposed the issue to God's truth and brought it out into the light, it can't stay hidden anymore. And if satan can't keep something hidden, his power over it and over that person will diminish.

In addition, I believe that there is a dynamic set in motion supernaturally when we come into right agreement with what God already knows to be true about ourselves. We are, in a sense, aligning ourselves with His will, which opens the door for Him to then be able to truly bring His full measure of healing and freedom into our lives when we admit to a sin that we've allowed to enter. When I work with my clients, one of the first things that I will encourage them to do is to confess out anything that may be weighing them down that the enemy has been using to beat them up. Some people are not comfortable speaking such things aloud at first, and if not, I will simply have them start by writing things down on paper, and then later, if they are willing, to speak them aloud, so that they can release those burdens off themselves and feel the freedom that the release can bring.

I would submit that one of the main reasons—if not the main

reason—for confession is to keep ourselves out of denial. As we all know, it can become very easy to justify, rationalize, and minimize a serious issue in our lives. If we do this, we will be truly living in a type of deception, because we won't be seeing the truth of our lives for what it really is. Confession breaks denial and deception, and that is why it is such a crucial key to our healing process. We can't change what we don't acknowledge, and so therefore we have to go back to the very act of acknowledging the existence of a problem or an issue in our lives before we can begin to seek God for His transformational and healing power!

day #22 refuge

refuge

Guard my soul and deliver me; do not let me be ashamed,
for I take refuge in You.
~ Psalm 25:20 ~

…The Words BEHIND the Word…

What does it mean for God to be our refuge…or for us to take refuge in Him? What it meant for David in Psalm 25 was that he could then entreat upon God to guard his soul and deliver him. Since our souls include our emotions, this in an area where we likely have been hurt and need God's healing touch. Now, to take refuge in God is not some casual, "feel-good" type of activity. David actually *completely* ran to God for refuge. In the Hebrew language, the text for "I take refuge" is written in the 'qal perfect verbal tense', which is just a fancy way of stating that David actively chose to take refuge in the Lord and that he performed the action until it was complete (thus perfect). David didn't half heart-edly take refuge in God; rather he chose to fully do it. Why did he do this? Because David knew what it meant to have God as his refuge, because if he didn't, he was exposing his soul to the onslaught of his enemies.

The word for "refuge" is *chasah* which carries the fundamental meaning of *to flee for protection,* and it therefore means *to take refuge, to trust in, or to hope in.* When we look at the word "guard", it is from the word *shamar* which means *to guard, to keep safe or preserve, to protect, to watch over, or to hedge about.* Therefore, a place of refuge in the Lord is a place of protection whereby God watches over us and keeps us safe. And watch He does, for if we look at Psalm 18:2, David says, "The Lord is my rock and my fortress and my deliverer, my God, my rock, in whom I take refuge; my shield and the horn of my salvation, my stronghold." That's a verse that packs a powerful punch because it shows that when we choose to take refuge in God, He is our rock, our fortress, our deliverer, the horn of our salvation (which is a sign of strength) *and* our stronghold. Fort Knox couldn't hold a candle to how strong and secure God is!

When we sense that we are entering areas that might hurt us, we need to run to God and rest in His watchful, protective care. In fact, "He shall cover thee with His feathers, and under His wings shalt thou trust: His truth shall be thy shield and buckler" (Psalm 91:4, KJV). As a mother bird jealously guards her young, so shall the Lord of Hosts guard us under His wings as we choose to flee to Him for protection and abide in His truth which will be a mighty shield in our hands.

...<u>Now That I Know It, How Do I Live It?</u>...

...*refuge*

Scripture tells us that God Himself is our refuge and our hiding place! This is an awesome concept when we look at what this really means for us. The God of the Universe wants us to run to *Him* when we need comfort and relief from the problems of this world. We can take refuge under the shelter of His strong and mighty wings when we need to. The strengthening and renewal that we receive when we let the Lord shelter us can be a very healing time in our lives.

When we take refuge in God, we are surrounded by His comforting presence. We allow ourselves to feel and experience the comfort that only He is capable of giving. Also, in this silent refuge, it is much easier to hear the Lord's still, small voice as He speaks words of reassurance and encouragement to our weary hearts. So much can be learned in the silence of God's presence. So much can be gained from merely sitting still under His protective wings. When we choose to take our refuge in God—instead of trying to find it in other people or in other situations—the Lord then gives us His "hidden treasures in darkness", as His word promises. There are blessings kept by Him just for us when we meet Him in the darkness. We open ourselves up to Him when we take refuge in Him: we allow Him to speak into our lives, impart His wisdom to us, provide us with the supernatural strength that we need to face life, shine His gentle light on the hidden chambers of our hearts that He alone can see, and also allow us to place our cares in His capable hands and lay our head back into His gentle arms.

Seeking refuge in God does not require a special prayer or formula; it is a simple act of our will which says, in effect, that we want to hide ourselves in Him. Once we decide that that's what we desire to do, we need only believe that it has been done, and we can now be hidden in Him as He ministers to us in all of the ways that He knows we need at that very moment. Sometimes in life we make things much harder than they really need to be; oftentimes we try to find resolution to our problems all by ourselves; or we feel that we need to figure it all out, and fix it alone; or that when we are truly exhausted and are running on empty, that somehow we should try to pick ourselves up by our bootstraps and trudge on anyway. The Lord is saying that He is there for us in these very situations, so that we *don't* adopt the impression that we have to do everything, all on our own, all of the time! There is much emphasis in our society on self-sufficiency and independence; however, I believe that the Lord would have us as His people be much more dependent—dependent upon Him for our safe hiding place...our refuge.

day #23 love

love

So that Christ may dwell in your hearts through faith; and that you, being rooted and grounded in love, may be able to comprehend with all the saints what is the breadth and length and height and depth [of His love].
~ Ephesians 3:17-18 ~

...The Words BEHIND the Word...

Many of us have probably heard about the *agape* love of God early in our Christian life. If we become truly rooted and grounded in His love, it will bring so much healing into our lives. Since God has created us with the need of being filled by His love, it becomes important for us to understand the love of God. The New Testament word *agape* means *love, affectionate regard, or goodwill* and when referring to God's love, it is God's willful direction toward man. *Agape* is derived from the verb *agapao* which means *to love, to esteem* and it indicates an inclination of the will and finding one's joy in something or someone. Outside of the New Testament, the word *agapao* was generally used in classical Greek writings as a synonym for *phileo*, which conveys the idea of a warm or fond affection. In the New Testament, *agapao* takes on a special significance where it refers to the love of God or the way of life based upon it. In almost every instance that these words are used, they speak of God's relationship with man. God's love is forgiving and sacrificial, yet it is also a love whereby God does what He knows is best for us and not necessarily what we desire. *God loves us because He willfully chooses to and He finds joy in loving us!*

In Ephesians 3:17, the Apostle Paul wanted the Ephesian believers to have the love of Christ dwell in their hearts through the means of faith. It is this faith in Jesus whereby we become children of God. The Greek word for dwell is *katoikeo* which is from *kata*, meaning *down from, down in, or down upon,* and *oikeo*, meaning *to dwell.* Therefore, it means *to dwell down in* and it indicates a durable or fixed dwelling. If Christ's love has taken residence in our hearts, it becomes to us a firm foundation and it is what we become rooted in. The picture that is portrayed is *that of a solid base that has been placed and laid down with a strong root system intermingled within the foundation.* As this happens, we will begin to comprehend, or literally take down into us, how Christ's love extends higher than the highest heaven, lower than the lowest hell, and spreads out across our horizon. It is this understanding of God's love where we begin to experience healing, for we know that whatever mountain or valley we are facing, God's love is abiding with us. It is this love that we will be experiencing throughout eternity. As Paul says in 1 Corinthians 13:13, "But now faith, hope, love, abide these three; but the greatest of these is love." Once we are in heaven, both our faith and hope in Christ have been fulfilled, but the love of God is something we will be experiencing forever!

...Now That I Know It, How Do I Live It?...

... love

We so often hear the term "unconditional love" today. I think that it is the heart cry of many to be able to experience unconditional love, but I also believe that it is much more difficult to demonstrate this kind of love than we may think. Christ demonstrated unconditional love perfectly, because He is Love. No one needed to earn His love; His love was never based upon performance or favors or anything that we as human beings have managed to introduce into the concept of unconditional love. Love requires selflessness in a person, and because of this, I believe that it is difficult for many of us to truly love the way Christ would have us to, because so much of what we are programmed with in society—not to mention by our own carnal nature and satan's lies—seems to focus mainly on the romantic aspect of love, the "me-first" love, and the fact that love is portrayed as a way to get our own needs met, instead of the reality of it, which is to meet the need of others without regard to our own.

The Lord will often use a marriage as the foundation upon which to teach each spouse about unconditional love, as it is a perfect venue through which lessons like these can be learned. This doesn't, however, mean that learning how to love unconditionally within the context of a marriage is all fun and games! Many of the couples I see at my practice struggle greatly in this area, and they are certainly not alone. It is a crucifying of our own flesh that needs to take place in many cases as we learn to put our spouse's needs before our own, and to make decisions for their best interests instead of always for our own. "Preferring one another in love" is how Scripture instructs us to conduct ourselves in this area of marriage.

As we begin to see that by serving others in love, we are also serving Christ Himself, it becomes a bit more eye-opening as to why the Lord puts so much emphasis on the importance of the love that we demonstrate and willingly give in our relationships. Love builds up, and in a hurting world where so many know of love in "name only", an act of love demonstrated can communicate so much to a person's heart, and bring encouragement and hope that there are still those that choose to be vessels for God's love to flow through. As we face each new day, we can pause and ask the Lord to provide us with opportunity to demonstrate His love to those in need, especially those right within our own families.

day #24 humility

humility

God is opposed to the proud, but gives grace to the humble.
Therefore humble yourselves under the mighty hand of God,
that He may exalt you at the proper time.
~ 1 Peter 5:5b-6 ~

…The Words BEHIND the Word…

Humility is not a terribly popular concept in this day and age! People in the world are so often taught to try to build themselves up by taking pride in themselves and in their accomplishments. Thus, humility might even be seen as something to be avoided. In fact, this is exactly how the ancient Greeks viewed humility. The Greek word for humility, *tapeinos*, has the meaning of *low, humble, or modest* and it indicates that one is low in attitude or social position, or low in the attitude of the mind. To the ancient Greek mind, *tapeinos* was looked at as something shameful, lowly, or that which needs to be overcome. This is quite the opposite to the view that Scripture has of humility.

In 1 Peter 5:5, which is a reference back to Proverbs 3:34, we are told that "God opposes the proud, but gives grace to the humble." The Greek word for "opposes" is *antitasso* which is a compound of the words *anti*, meaning *against*, and *tasso*, meaning *to arrange*. Thus, it has the meaning of *arranging against, to resist, or to oppose*. It is actually a military term meaning to set an army against, or to arrange in a battle order. If we want to be on God's side, on His army, we surely don't want to be proud! The word for "proud", *huperephanos*, is another compound word formed from *huper* which means *over, above* and *phaino* meaning *to shine, to show*. Therefore, it is one who tries to shine above the rest, one who seeks the spotlight and who wants to be noticed. We are instructed to let our light shine before men – but this should be God's light that is reflecting off of us, not our own light that we are trying to shine!

Humility is a choice, and God won't force us to make it. And the circumstances of our life that we find ourselves in can, at times, make it fairly easy to walk in pride, but if we continue to lift ourselves up, we'll eventually fall and with that falling we're bound to end up hurt! If God is opposing us if we are proud, than what does He want us to do? We are to choose to humble ourselves under His hand. This choice, in fact, is a command, for it is written in the imperative tense in the Greek. If we choose to think of ourselves in a proper light, as those who need God, and know that our flesh is weak, God will, out of His mercy and love, exalt us at the proper time. This exalting is the word *hupsoo* meaning *to raise high, elevate, or lift up*. God does this at just the right time that we need it, as the phrase "at the proper time" comes from the word *kairos* which means *a season of time, the critical moment*. If we bring this all together, we can see that pride leads to hurt, as we are viewing ourselves in a way that is not consistent with God's view of us. When we view ourselves as God sees us, this opens the door for God to bring His healing power into our hearts at the exact time we need it.

...<u>Now That I Know It, How Do I Live It?</u>...
...humilty

One of the ways that we can know that we are operating inside of God's will for our lives is if we maintain a "teachable spirit." A teachable spirit is built upon a foundation of true humility. When a person is "teachable", it means that their heart is soft enough to receive feedback and input, even though the feedback or input might sting at first, because they know it will be for their ultimate good. They have reached a place of emotional and spiritual maturity in which they are sufficiently grounded in who they are in Christ, and as such, can remain open to new ideas and receive suggestions for improvement if needed. And in order for a person to retain a teachable spirit, they have to remain humble.

Humility acknowledges that all of us in the human race are fallen, have sinned, and have come short of the glory of God. And knowing this, it keeps life in perspective in the sense that no one person is "above" or better than another; Scripture tells us that God is no respecter of persons in this sense. When we realize this, we can begin to develop a fuller appreciation for just how much God loves us and lavishes His grace upon us, even though we are in this fallen condition. The Lord is familiar with all the struggles, challenges, and temptations we will face in this life, and one of the keys to having victory over them is to refuse to operate in pride, but instead choose humility.

To simplify this truth, pride in essence says "Look at me", whereas humility in essence says "Don't look at me." A humble person has achieved the proper perspective of himself as related to a Holy God, and doesn't try to self-exalt or self-promote because of it. Pride, on the other hand, seeks out the accolades, the recognition, and, oftentimes, the spotlight. We are told in Scripture that pride goes before a fall. Why is this? It's not because we serve an indignant God who gains some enjoyment in watching us land on our face, but rather He allows the fall out of His great love for, and mercy upon, us as His children. He knows that if He were to continue to sit back and watch us go through life in a prideful manner, that we eventually would find ourselves in very dire circumstances, likely even isolated and friend-less. The Lord wants to spare us from that agony, so He will try to get our attention early on and make us aware of the fact (if we'll let Him!) that we need to lay our prideful ways down and instead choose humility.

A good rule of thumb regarding humility is to make a habit of humbling ourselves—before God has to do it for us! It is never fun when we have been walking in pride and haven't caught ourselves; when the Lord intervenes, we often wish we would've been much more cognizant of our heart attitude and adjusted it accordingly to line up with humility! We must be careful to not walk in "false humility" either; this is self-serving and accomplishes no good. Walking in humility not only keeps our hearts soft, but it has many other healing benefits in our daily lives as well, including helping to keep us grateful, honest, sensitive, and nonjudgmental. Humility gives us a balanced perspective on what life—and our role in it—is all about!

deliverance

deliverance

Who hath delivered us from the power of darkness, and hath
translated us into the kingdom of His dear Son
~ Colossians 1:13 (KJV) ~

...The Words BEHIND the Word...

The word of God packs a powerful punch and Colossians 1:13 is no exception. It really describes to us what happens during any type of true deliverance from the kingdom of darkness: where we were, the process that moved us, and where we are now. In this passage, God the Father is the One doing the delivering and that helps us to remember that it is always God or His authority that does the delivering, not anything of ourselves.

Rhuomai is the word translated "delivered" and it comes from the Greek word *rhuo* which means *to draw, or to drag along the ground,* and it thus means *to deliver, rescue, to draw or snatch from danger.* It also has the fundamental meaning of *to draw to oneself.* From this we can see that God rescued us, or drew us to Himself, and this rescuing was from the power, *exousia*, of darkness. Those that possess *exousia* have *the power, permission, or the right and authority to do something.* This is why it is so important for us to abstain from sin because when we don't, it gives the realm of darkness the legal right to exercise authority over that area of our lives.

It is these same *exousia* that we wrestle against in Ephesians 6:12 (translated "powers"). Since the realm of darkness already exercises authority over this world, we certainly don't need to offer them anything else in our own lives!

At the time of our salvation, the right that satan had to keep us in his kingdom was broken. Thus, God translated us (*methistano* in the Greek) from the kingdom of darkness into the kingdom of light governed by Jesus. Since *methistano* is from the words *meta* meaning *together with or change of location*, and *histemi* meaning *to stand*, God literally caused us *to stand together with Him in a different place*! This is what happens to us whenever God brings us through the healing process of deliverance – He moves us out from under the authority of darkness and causes us to stand together with Him in the kingdom of His dear Son (literally "the Son of His love")! Now, if we think back to our salvation experience, what was it that caused God to deliver us? It was our act of repentance. Sometimes we may cry out for God to deliver us from a sinful behavior and He may do it out of His grace, but He really desires that we repent of that behavior so that He can perform a more complete and lasting deliverance. As we work together with and in agreement with God, the shadows of darkness will fade and we will come away healed and delivered...now standing in His kingdom of light.

...<u>Now That I Know It, How Do I Live It?</u>...

...*deliverance*

There seems to be some level of confusion about the whole concept of deliverance amongst many in our churches today. This is not surprising, because it is not a simple or necessarily an easy area to understand. Deliverance is, however, a very important aspect of the healing process, and individuals can at times experience tremendous freedom and release from issues or strongholds that may have plagued them for as far back as they can remember. Many components come into play when we speak of deliverance, so let's take a brief look at some common situations which might necessitate spiritual warfare of this kind.

First of all, if it is believed that a deliverance might be needed, it is helpful to examine possible "entry points" or "legal ground" that the enemy has had in being able to gain access to a person's life. (It is my belief that a Christian cannot be "demon possessed" because Christ is our owner, but rather that he or she can be demonized or demonically oppressed.) Legal ground can consist of (but is not limited to) previous dabbling in any aspect of the occult (satan's domain), generational sin or family-line assignments, abuse by another person, ongoing sin without repentance, spiritual links or "soul ties" to another person, being bound in a covenant relationship with a non-believer, and *unhealed wounds*, just to provide a partial list. Unhealed wounds may not seem to be an obvious or even valid demonic entry point in a person's life, but unfortunately, it can be if it is left unaddressed for long enough. I commonly use the phrase in my practice that "demons are like rats to garbage." Once the mess is cleaned up, the demons shouldn't have a reason to come back. The same thing happens with our emotional wounds. If we've harbored bitterness, unforgiveness, or resentment towards another, these wounds can then become "infected", so to speak. Unaddressed wounds are highly desirable territory for the enemy to come in and try to claim legal ground, because the individual with these wounds has held on to them, nurtured them, and perhaps has refused to give them over to the Lord and take the necessary healing steps of forgiveness. In addition, if a demon is commanded to leave, but the emotional mess is not "cleaned up", the demon can immediately return. Although it can at times be difficult to accurately pinpoint the exact reasons for demonic activity in a person's life, these are representative of some common places to begin with when dealing in this area.

I personally believe firmly in the combination of healing prayer (God-directed inner healing) and deliverance; I believe that they are most effective in a person's life when used in conjunction with each other. For example, if a person chooses to ask God to search his or her heart, and then responds in an obedient manner by forgiving someone, or doing whatever the Lord may have shown him or her to do, then at times the demonic will leave on their own because the "emotional mess" has now been cleaned up. Other times, there will be much more exploration and seeking God's wisdom and direction that will be necessary in order for a full deliverance and healing to take place. Some demonic may have legal ground that is different than what you might guess (some at times may even be there without legal ground as well!), and some emotional wounds are not what they first appear to be either. For this reason, it is vital that we put the Lord in charge of this whole process, as He is the Omniscient One who can guide and direct by His wisdom when it comes to dealing with the healing of deep emotional wounds and deliverance!

day #26 **yielded**

yielded

Neither yield ye your members as instruments of unrighteousness unto sin: but yield yourselves unto God, as those that are alive from the dead, and your members as instruments of righteousness unto God.
~ Romans 6:13 (KJV) ~

…The Words BEHIND the Word…

If we take a look at the Greek word for "yield", *paristemi*, we'll get a good picture of what it actually means to yield ourselves to God. *Paristemi* is a compound verb formed from the word *para* meaning *along side or near* and *histemi* meaning *to place or to stand*. Thus, the word for yield actually means *to cause to stand near or along side* and it conveys the idea of one being placed in the presence of another. In Romans 6:13, the Apostle Paul uses the imperative verb tense, which is a command. In other words, we are instructed to be the ones who do the yielding to God – He doesn't force us to yield to Him! In fact, when we yield to God, we are placing ourselves in a position that is standing near Him – and there is no better place to stand than in His Presence.

We are also commanded to NOT yield ourselves, our members, to sin. The word translated "neither" is the word *medeis* a compound from the word *mede* meaning *and not*, and *heis* which means *one*. Therefore it means *not even one*, so we should never yield a

118

single part of us to sin! This phase is also a conditional negative, which means it is dependent upon something else – which in this case is our will. So what happens when we do yield our members to sin? Our members, which is *melos* in the Greek, become instruments, *hoplon*, of unrighteousness. The *melos* refers to *our limbs, that which is of the body, or those members that are our desires and passions.* A *hoplon* is an *instrument or tool for preparing something* and it is most often used to describe *instruments or weapons of warfare.* When we yield ourselves to sin, that is to place ourselves standing on satan's side, we actually become weapons of warfare for the enemy!

Jesus stated in John 10:10 that, "The thief comes only to steal and kill and destroy; I came that they may have life, and have it abundantly." If we want healing in our lives, yielding to sin is not the means to accomplish it. We'll end up on the enemy's side where his goal is to bring about our destruction which includes killing, *thuo*, and destroying, *appolumi*, meaning *to cause to perish, to render useless.* Interestingly, *thuo* has the meaning of *to kill and offer in sacrifice.* This is where the enemy wants us, in a place whereby our lives have been rendered useless as we sin and sacrifice our lives to the flesh. God, on the contrary, has come to give us *life*, which is the Greek word *zoe* in John 10:10. *Zoe* is the life that Jesus has come to give us; this word is always used whenever eternal life is referred to in the New Testament. This word is full of so much hope and healing, as this type of life is truly a life that is fully alive, not one that has yielded to the flesh; rather, it is one that has yielded to God. As we yield to God it is for our benefit and we experience the life, the *zoe*, that Jesus intended for us here on earth and then fully with Him in eternity.

...<u>Now That I Know It, How Do I Live It?</u>...

...*yielded*

Yielded...this is really an issue of just how much of our heart we are willing to give over to God so that He can work in our lives in His fullest measure. Just as a "Yield" sign is clearly different from a "Stop" sign, the Lord isn't asking us to stop being who we are; He's just asking that we *yield* who we are to Him! We hold the power to make the choice here of how much of our lives we are willing to surrender to God; as I've previously mentioned, God is a gentleman and He will not override our free will or force us to do something that we don't want to.

Another way to view the concept of being yielded to God is the following: Picture in your mind a 3-legged stool. Each of the 3 legs represents something different. The first leg represents Christ as Savior—He has saved you. The second leg represents Christ as Lord—He owns you. The third leg represents Christ as King—He rules you. We need to allow Christ to play all 3 roles in our lives if this stool is to remain steady and balanced. If even one of the legs is a little shorter than the others, the stool will be wobbly and unstable. So it is always in our best interest if we allow the Lord to fully be all aspects to us: Savior, Lord, and King. Most of us don't have much difficulty with allowing Him to be Savior—especially after He's saved us! But it is the other 2 roles that can be more challenging for us to fully submit to, because each of them requires that we yield—or surrender—more of ourselves and our lives over to Him. Yielding to God in all 3 capacities really is a learning process, because none of us will do it perfectly all the time. We need to take it one step at a time. And sometimes, we will yield an area of our lives over to the Lord and leave it with Him at the foot of the cross, but then a few minutes later we'll sneak back over to it, pick it up again, and try to handle it ourselves! But that's okay because God already knows that it will happen like this at times, and the main thing to remember is that practice makes perfect—keep placing it back at His feet, even if you continue to go and pick it up again. Just keep practicing yielding until you can take it there and permanently keep it there!

The more of ourselves that we are willing to yield to God, the more blessed—and healthy!—we will be, because He knows that we need to let Him own us as Lord and rule over us as King, in order for us to reach our maximum potential in Him, to develop and mature our character the way He wants us to, and to remain under His authority in all possible ways so that we will always fall under His umbrella of protection over our lives...which is present when we are submitted and yielded to Him. He knows that we will have the greatest measure of joy and peace when we live this way, because we will be seated firmly on a "stool" that is strong, stable and balanced—and as a result, our emotional and spiritual health will be brought into balance as well!

day #27 steadfast

steadfast

Therefore, my beloved brethren, be steadfast, immovable, always abounding in the work of the Lord, knowing that your toil is not in vain in the Lord.
~ 1 Corinthians 15:58 ~

...The Words BEHIND the Word...

In 1 Corinthians 15:35-57, the Apostle Paul presents the glorious hope that we have in the resurrection of our mortal bodies into bodies that will live forever. This is all possible because of Jesus' victory over sin, which brought about a triumph over death and the grave. He concludes this passage with verse 58 which relates to us the importance of continuing in the Lord's work so that others may too experience the same glories that we will. Now, he doesn't want us to "sort of" keep working, or to "give it a good try" – no, he wants us to be steadfast and immovable! Paul knows and the enemy knows that it takes an almost stubborn resolve to continue on and not falter because there will be fruits of our labor. The same is true of any battle – we need to press through no matter what and remain firm, since oftentimes our healing is dependant upon our resolve to be healed.

Paul uses the word *hedraios* for "steadfast", which originally referred to *standing steady on the ground*, and it is a word that is derived from *hedra* which means *a seat or a chair*. Therefore, the word came to mean *someone who is seated*, but its later usage came to mean *firm, steadfast, unshakeable or stable*. We can almost think of it as referring to someone who has found their spot of stability and says, "I'm not moving!" The word that is translated "immovable" is the Greek word *ametakinetos* which is formed from the words *a*, meaning *not*, *meta*, meaning *together with or change of location*, and *kineo* meaning *to move*, which is where we get our word "kinetic" from, as in "kinetic energy." If we put this all together it means *not moving in order to change location or position; unmovable or firm*. So what is Paul telling us here? He is telling us *to be seated in a firm, stable position and to remain there and never move from it*! Now that's resolve!

He also goes on to say that our toil, which is *kopos*, meaning *beating, wailing, or grieving until it brings about weariness*, is not in vain. The word for "vain" is *kenos*, which is defined as *empty, hollow, fruitless, or useless*. God will make sure that the fruits of our labor will amount to something and not leave us empty-handed. So, whether we are laboring for Christ, abiding to keep His word, or seeking His healing, we can rest assured that if we do it with resolve and make up in our minds that we are not moving from what we are trying to accomplish, God will ensure that our efforts and toil will not be in vain.

...<u>Now That I Know It, How Do I Live It?</u>...

...steadfast

Being steadfast in our Christian walk is one of the best ways to avoid becoming doubleminded in what we believe and in what we practice. When we think of someone who is steadfast, we think of someone who is any one of or any combination of the following: unwavering, resolute, persistent, committed, dedicated, firm, reliable, consistent, faithful, or devoted. Imagine if we were able to have a track record in our walk with the Lord that displayed the vast majority of these qualities, the vast majority of the time! In a case like that, it could definitely be argued that we'd be doing fairly well! The reality is, unfortunately, that this would be much more the exception than the rule. Many of us base our decision to spend time with God (in His Word, in prayer, in worship, and so on) on whether we *feel* like doing it or not at that point in time. And because feelings are extremely fickle, and they seem to change with the direction of the wind, we will rarely show any consistency using this approach in our time spent with God...the most valuable way that any of us can possibly spend our time!

The good news is that we can learn how to become steadfast, through the power of the Holy Spirit. We can learn how to develop this important character trait. And in order to learn how to cultivate this trait, we need to understand that we will need to die to our flesh to some degree in order to become steadfast. Why? Because the flesh tends very strongly towards instant gratification: doing something when we feel like it and not doing it when we don't, giving up if something becomes too challenging or takes too long, making half-hearted attempts at things, and wanting to live by our own rules, even if those rules are dictated by laziness only! But when we choose to deny our flesh whatever it is demanding from us at the moment, and choose instead to persist faithfully in what we know God has shown us to do, the Lord will send us His supernatural strength and resolve to stay the course and help strengthen our commitment and devotion to proceed with what He's asked of us.

Developing a steadfast character does not happen overnight, of course. But each time we take one step (however small) to perse-vere in our faith, we will make our ability to remain steadfast a little stronger. On the flip side, each time we choose to react according to how we feel or give up on something, our flesh will get a little stronger. *Whatever side we feed gets stronger!* So let's try to purpose in our hearts to cultivate steadfastness in our lives, and then watch for how the Lord will honor and bless our efforts.

day #28 **balance**

balance

Be well balanced (temperate, sober of mind), be vigilant and cautious at all times; for that enemy of yours, the devil, roams around like a lion roaring [in fierce hunger], seeking someone to seize upon and devour. Withstand him; be firm in faith [against his onset—rooted, established, strong, immovable, and deter-mined], knowing that the same (identical) sufferings are appointed to your brotherhood (the whole body of Christians) throughout the world.
~ 1 Peter 5:8-9 (AMP) ~

...The Words BEHIND the Word...

Maintaining balance is one of the essential elements of the Christian life. In a world that says, "grab all you can get", we see how material possessions can quickly get out of balance. However, being balanced covers all the areas of our lives, not just those of possessions, and can even extend into spiritual matters such as believing there is "a demon in every doorknob" or "there's no such thing as the devil." The Amplified version of the Bible presents additional insights in the words we read by expanding upon the original Hebrew and Greek languages. As such, the beginning of this passage is normally translated "be sober" in the majority of translations while the Amplified version renders it "be well balanced."

The word for "well balanced" comes from the word *nepho* which literally means *to be sober or not intoxicated,* but it also conveys the idea of a figurative sobriety where, because of the clarity of the mind, good judgment results and this leads to a preference for *moderation.* Therefore, *nepho* can mean *watchful, careful, sober-minded or well-balanced.* This is the first instruction that Peter gives us; however, he doesn't stop there as he also tells us to be "vigilant and cautious at all times." This is from the Greek word *gregoreuo* which is derived from *egeiro* meaning *to arise or to arouse as in rising from a sleep.* It thus has the meaning of *to watch, to refrain from sleep, to be alert, or to be mindful of dangers that may be lurking.* This is the same word that Jesus used with His disciples in the garden of Gethsemane when He asked them to "watch" while He went just beyond them to pray. In essence, He was telling them, "don't fall asleep because there are dangers lurking; be ready and alert for any surprise attack from the enemy so that you can defend yourself."

So why should we be watchful and alert? Because the devil is prowling around! The phrase "roams around" is from *peripateo* which is formed from *peri,* meaning *around, about* (which is used in our word "perimeter" meaning *around the edges*), and *pateo,* meaning to walk.

Therefore, the devil is literally walking around us, encircling us, seeking an opportunity in our lives to devour us! Literally, he wants to swallow us up since the word for "devour" is *katapino,* which is from *kata* meaning *down,* and *pino,* meaning *to drink.* Peter tells us to "resist" him which is *anthistemi,* formed from *anti,* meaning *against,* and *histemi,* meaning *to stand.* Therefore, we need to *stand against* the devil and his schemes to throw our lives out of balance, as balance will help keep us whole and give us solid ground on which to resist the devil and remain alert to his tactics!

...<u>Now That I Know It, How Do I Live It?</u>...

...balance

Living a balanced life is arguably one of the most crucial components for good emotional and spiritual health. Some people have a relatively easy time balancing the different aspects of their lives, but for most of us, it requires a lot of effort, focus and attention to stay in equilibrium! Scripture stresses the importance of staying balanced as well, because it is when we get out of balance in an area (or areas) of our lives that we become very easy prey for the enemy. Especially in a day and age where people seem to be busier than ever before, and are trying to juggle more balls in the air while simultaneously preventing them from being dropped, learning how to live a balanced life becomes even more of a necessity.

We are not necessarily hard-wired for balance; in fact, in some cases I tend to think we are hard-wired for extremes instead! We seem to either go off into one ditch or the other, and have a difficult time staying in the middle of the road. When this is the case, it takes fresh perspective and renewed energy to pull ourselves up and out of the ditch and set ourselves back on the central path again. It's much easier to get out of balance than we may think, mainly because there are so many areas that require us to stay on top of the balancing act. To name just a few: spending money, eating, watching television, sleeping, exercise, movies, internet time, working, sex, sports, even vacations! So, it's fairly easy to see that nearly every aspect of life is a potential area that can become out of balance. And, taken to even more of an extreme, these areas can wind up as addictions if they are left unchecked. An addiction is an area of bondage to which a person is a slave; addictions consume and control people's lives. This may be an extreme example to illustrate the importance of managing our lives in a balanced manner, but unfortunately the road from slight excess to full-blown addiction is much shorter and more slippery than many of us realize. Once someone's life has lost all balance and he or she is out of control, it can be a long and difficult uphill climb to reclaim that balance again.

It's important to remember also that satan doesn't care what he uses to destroy us; as long as he is able to, in fact, destroy. Temporarily spending a little more time or energy on something might not seem like any big deal at first, but we need to be alert and aware, because the enemy can snare us using very subtle tactics. Before too long, we may just find that a particular area or activity is beginning to take on a "life of its own", whereas at one point we controlled it, but now it seems to be controlling us.

The Holy Spirit is faithful when we ask Him to show us if there are any areas of our lives that are in danger of becoming out of balance; I believe we need to seek God on this issue quite frequently. The Spirit will help us make changes and keep our lives balanced and on track!

day #29 united

united

Teach me Your way, O LORD; I will walk in Your truth;
unite my heart to fear Your name.
~ Psalm 86:11 ~

...The Words BEHIND the Word...

United. Divided. Two words that are at opposite extremes. God wants us to be united with Him, for us to be united in heart, and for us to be united with our brothers and sisters in Christ. However, we know all too well how disagreements can possibly lead to division and discord. When it comes to being united to God, fundamentally it boils down to the issue of whether or not we will trust and obey God, and sometimes our choice not to obey comes out of our own fears. However, each time we choose not to obey Him, this can bring a division into our soul. Satan knows this all too well, for he knows that if he can persuade us not to obey God, this can lead to division. Jesus Himself said in Matthew 12:25, a "house divided against itself will not stand." The word for "house" is the Greek word *oikia* which means *a residence, building, or house.* Another word for "house" is *oikos* which generally refers to a person's possession, estate, and house. The Holy Spirit is being very specific here by using the word *oikia*. If our personal residence is divided, we will not be able *to stand fast, endure or persist,* for this is what the word *histemi*—translated "stand"—means. This relays to us the importance of being united in heart.

In Psalm 86:11, David requests of the Lord that He unite his (David's) heart. The word for "unite" is *yachad* which means *to join or unite,* and it carries with it the idea of making something one. If we look into the actual Hebrew verbal construction of the word "unite", it is what is termed a 'piel imperative.' That's somewhat of a mouthful, but if we break it down we can get a better perspective. The 'piel stem', as it's called, refers to an established state of being, without being concerned as to how that state came about. The imperative, quite simply, is a command. Obviously, David cannot command God to do anything, but by using this verbal tense he is saying, in essence, "God, I implore you and desire greatly that you unite my heart – and I'm not concerned with how you do it, I just want you to do it!" David knew how important it was for his heart to be united, for he knew that if his heart was united, he will then fear God which will keep him from sin. If David's heart was divided, he knew that he could more easily fall into sin.

The importance of being united is also repeatedly demonstrated in the New Testament. In his letter to the Colossians, Paul states in 3:14, "beyond all these things put on love, which is the perfect bond of unity." Here, the word "unity" is *sundesmos* which has its roots in *sun,* meaning *together,* and *deo,* meaning *to bind.* This word then means *that which binds together,* and Paul is stating that love is the perfect bind! *Teleiotes* from *teleios* is the word "perfect" and it carries the meaning of a goal or purpose that is achieved, or coming to the complete end of a purpose. John tells us in 1 John 4:18 that "perfect love casts out fear", where *teleios* is the underlying word for "perfect." We have now come full circle, for if fear can cause us division, God's desire is for us to be clothed with His love which casts (*ballo* which literally means *to throw*) out the fears that we may have, and which will help us to fulfill one of God's main goals for our hearts—unity! Praise God for His work in us!

...<u>Now That I Know It, How Do I Live It?</u>...
...*united*

It's hard to emphasize enough the tremendous importance of cultivating a heart (and mind) that is *united* within ourselves. The Bible has much to say about this issue, because the Lord knows that we will never be able to have true and lasting peace or contentment if we are constantly wavering between two opinions, or pulled in two directions for the affections in our heart. James 1:8 clearly tells us that "A double minded man is unstable in all his ways" (KJV). When there is no stability of the heart or the mind, anything goes, and satan has a prime opportunity to enter the picture and add even more confusion to the current situation. When we are constantly trying to decide between one thing and another, and we don't use the resources available to us that could help us make a wise and informed choice, we end up spinning our wheels while the infrastructure begins to collapse inside. At this point, life can become quite complicated, confusing, even overwhelming, and we can begin to adapt some very unhealthy and detrimental patterns just in order to cope. Taken at an extreme, with regard to the field of mental health, if a person has been "split" for too long in mind and/or in heart, there is sometimes the potential for a diagnosis of schizophrenia in that individual (*schizo* meaning "split", and *phreneo* meaning "mind"). Literally, then, schizophrenics suffer from an actual splitting of the mind, and once the mind has been split to this degree, it is rare for it to spontaneously repair itself without major interventions and, primarily, God's healing power.

Our loving Lord does not want to see us have to go through all of the unnecessary turmoil that comes along with an inability to stay united in heart and mind, and that is why Psalm 86:11 strongly exhorts us to ask the Lord to "Teach me Your way, O LORD, I will walk in your truth: *unite my heart to fear Your Name.*" I believe that one of the keys He is showing us here in how to avoid walking in doublemindedness is to adopt a reverential fear for the awesome Name of God, and let this reverence for Him, and desire to please and obey Him, keep our hearts united toward Him instead of divided, where we can become very easy prey for the enemy.

Scripture also tells us that a house divided against itself cannot stand. This is very true, and many examples could be named here, including divorce, constant strife, polar opposite opinions with no willingness to compromise, child-against-parent disputes and so forth. Another type of "house" which we carry with us every day—the temple of the Holy Spirit—needs to be given just as much attention as the house of our family, because it all starts with "home base" – we have to remain united *within ourselves* out of reverential fear for God, and then we will hopefully be able to address those situations around us in which division is sprouting up as a cry for help!

day #30 acceptance
acceptance

Therefore, accept one another,
just as Christ also accepted us to the glory of God.
~ Romans 15:7 ~

...The Words BEHIND the Word...

One of the most comforting thoughts that we can meditate upon is that we are accepted by God. This is truly amazing because we have sinned and rebelled against God. But God had another plan – one that would bring us back into a right relationship with Him. It is this relationship with Him and His acceptance of us that forms one of the essential foundations of our lives, since we won't have to live out our lives searching for acceptance in someone or something else, because we know that we are already accepted by God!

We are told by Paul in his letter to the Romans that God has already accepted us, and in the same fashion, we are to accept others, specifically our fellow brothers and sisters in Christ. *Proslambano* is translated "accept", and it is taken from *pros* meaning *towards*, and *lambano* meaning *to take or to receive*, therefore it can be defined as *to take to oneself, to take with, or to receive into fellowship*. This is exactly what God did for us – He took us towards Himself that we might be received into His fellowship! Also, we don't have to continue to gain His acceptance, we already have it!

134

Without getting too technical, the Greek verb tense that is used for "accepted" is the 'aorist tense' which means that it is an action that happened at a specific point in time, usually in the past. Therefore, God's acceptance of us is a done deal – it occurred when we received (the word *lambano*) Christ as our Savior (see John 1:12).

Now, for us as believers we are commanded to *continually or repeatedly* accept our fellow believers. The same Greek word is used, but it is used with a different verb tense. The Lord knows that we as humans can become fickle and judgmental so He stresses to us the importance of continually accepting one another in Christ. Of course, He is not telling us to be accepting of sin, but to accept our fellow believers who are in various stages of Christian maturity. Paul tells us in Romans 14:1, "Now accept the one who is weak in faith, but not for the purpose of passing judgment on his opinions", where he uses the word *proslambano* for "accept." If one believer chooses to abstain from certain foods while another believer does not, both need to accept one another! It is oftentimes these small matters that lead to divisions and hurts among the body of Christ for which we may spend wasted time in arguments and strife. God accepts both believers' positions (see Romans 14:3) as long as both are doing it 'as unto the Lord'. So let's know who we are in Christ, our position of acceptance in Him, and extend that same acceptance to others.

...<u>Now That I Know It, How Do I Live It?</u>...

...*acceptance*

One of the most important needs of human beings is to know that they are accepted. This need for acceptance is so strong, in fact, that people will go to great lengths to find it. Taken at an extreme example, at the heart of gang membership is a need to be accepted and to belong. So often we stand in judgment of others, and probably even more often in judgment of other Christians, when what each of us actually wants is just to be accepted. Christ met people right where they were at. He didn't expect things of the people He ministered to that He knew they weren't yet able to give. There is so much rejection that dictates peoples' behavior, and this is nothing new; it has been this way since Adam and Eve after the fall. When we don't feel that we can truly be ourselves around other people, for fear that if they really knew us that then they'd reject us, is one of the major relational roadblocks that affects relationships of all kinds every day. We want to know that those closest to us—family and friends in particular—will accept us unconditionally. Sadly enough, this is rarely the case; much acceptance seems to be related to performance and achievement, not just for who a person is in his or her own right. Unconditional acceptance—acceptance without judgment—is a very tall order to fill. No one demonstrates it perfectly, and because of this, many people get hurt and are then tempted to try to find other venues for acceptance and other ways to fit in and belong.

Some people, when fearing or expecting rejection, will go so far as to sabotage a relationship on purpose before the other party has a chance to reject them first. I call this in my practice a type of "pre-emptive rejection"; in other words, choosing to reject someone else before they reject you, because it won't seem to be as painful. This is an example of our desire to self-protect, instead of letting God do it for us, and it accomplishes nothing but the building up of walls, which prove to be very difficult to tear down.

When we desire to be accepted by another person or a group of people, we are placed into a somewhat vulnerable position. In a sense, they hold all the cards as to whether we will be deemed acceptable or "worthy" to join them. This is potentially a very powerless and unstable place to be emotionally, because all of the power has been given over to these others by whom the person is seeking acceptance. I'll frequently counsel clients to not give all their power away in this manner; it eventually leads to a very unhealthy relationship for all parties involved, because neither being powerless nor being *all*-powerful is a balanced perspective to a relationship.

The best place—and the first place!—to seek acceptance is to get it from God. Why? Because His word states that we already have it anyway! Romans 15:7 states directly that we are accepted by God, and John 17:19 tells us that we belong to God! The very things we search so hard for in the world, God has already provided for us because He knew that we would need them! Knowing that we are accepted by God can be the solid rock beneath our feet that we need when it comes to our self-worth and self-esteem issues...not only should we have the above verses, and others like them, committed to memory, but we need to begin to walk them out in our everyday lives through the power of the Holy Spirit!

~ Journal and Study Notes ~

compassion

How can I allow the L\ord to use this Healing Word in my heart and in my life?

_____

_____

_____

_____

_____

_____

_____

_____

_____

_____

_____

_____

_____

_____

_____

_____

_____

_____

_____

_____

_____

_____

_____

_____

_____

_____

DATE:_____

compassion...
(continued)

contentment

How can I allow the LORD to use this Healing Word in my heart and in my life?

_____
_____
_____
_____
_____
_____
_____
_____
_____
_____
_____
_____
_____
_____
_____
_____
_____
_____
_____
_____
_____
_____
_____
_____
_____
_____
_____
_____
_____

DATE:_____

contentment...
(continued)

forgiveness

How can I allow the Lord to use this Healing Word in my heart and in my life?

_____

_____

_____

_____

_____

_____

_____

_____

_____

_____

_____

_____

_____

_____

_____

_____

_____

_____

_____

_____

_____

_____

_____

_____

_____

_____

_____

_____

_____

DATE:_____

forgiveness...
(continued)

truth

How can I allow the L<small>ORD</small> to use this Healing Word in my heart and in my life?

_____
_____
_____
_____
_____
_____
_____
_____
_____
_____
_____
_____
_____
_____
_____
_____
_____
_____
_____
_____
_____
_____
_____
_____
_____
_____
_____

DATE:_____

truth...
(continued)

freedom

*How can I allow the L*ORD *to use this Healing Word in my heart and in my life?*

_____
_____
_____
_____
_____
_____
_____
_____
_____
_____
_____
_____
_____
_____
_____
_____
_____
_____
_____
_____
_____
_____
_____
_____
_____
_____
_____

DATE:_____

freedom...
(continued)

restoration

How can I allow the Lord to use this Healing Word in my heart and in my life?

_____
_____
_____
_____
_____
_____
_____
_____
_____
_____
_____
_____
_____
_____
_____
_____
_____
_____
_____
_____
_____
_____
_____
_____
_____
_____

DATE:_____

restoration...
(continued)

comfort

How can I allow the L<small>ORD</small> to use this Healing Word in my heart and in my life?

_____

_____

_____

_____

_____

_____

_____

_____

_____

_____

_____

_____

_____

_____

_____

_____

_____

_____

_____

_____

_____

_____

_____

_____

_____

DATE:_____

comfort...
(continued)

peace

How can I allow the L<small>ORD</small> to use this Healing Word in my heart and in my life?

_____
_____
_____
_____
_____
_____
_____
_____
_____
_____
_____
_____
_____
_____
_____
_____
_____
_____
_____
_____
_____
_____
_____
_____
_____
_____
_____

DATE:_____

peace...
(continued)

grace

*How can I allow the L*ORD *to use this Healing Word in my heart and in my life?*

_____
_____
_____
_____
_____
_____
_____
_____
_____
_____
_____
_____
_____
_____
_____
_____
_____
_____
_____
_____
_____
_____
_____
_____
_____
_____

DATE:_____

grace...
(continued)

faith

How can I allow the LORD to use this Healing Word in my heart and in my life?

_____

_____

_____

_____

_____

_____

_____

_____

_____

_____

_____

_____

_____

_____

_____

_____

_____

_____

_____

_____

_____

_____

_____

DATE:_____

faith...
(continued)

repentance

How can I allow the LORD to use this Healing Word in my heart and in my life?

_____
_____
_____
_____
_____
_____
_____
_____
_____
_____
_____
_____
_____
_____
_____
_____
_____
_____
_____
_____
_____
_____
_____
_____
_____
_____

DATE:_____

repentance...
(continued)

hope

How can I allow the Lord *to use this Healing Word in my heart and in my life?*

_____
_____
_____
_____
_____
_____
_____
_____
_____
_____
_____
_____
_____
_____
_____
_____
_____
_____
_____
_____
_____
_____
_____
_____
_____
_____
_____
_____

DATE:_____

hope...
(continued)

trust

How can I allow the LORD to use this Healing Word in my heart and in my life?

_____

_____

_____

_____

_____

_____

_____

_____

_____

_____

_____

_____

_____

_____

_____

_____

_____

_____

_____

_____

_____

_____

_____

_____

_____

_____

_____

DATE:_____

trust...
(continued)

_____
_____
_____
_____
_____
_____
_____
_____
_____
_____
_____
_____
_____
_____
_____
_____
_____
_____
_____
_____
_____
_____
_____
_____
_____
_____
_____
_____

gratitude

How can I allow the LORD to use this Healing Word in my heart and in my life?

_____
_____
_____
_____
_____
_____
_____
_____
_____
_____
_____
_____
_____
_____
_____
_____
_____
_____
_____
_____
_____
_____
_____
_____
_____
_____

DATE:_____

gratitude...
(continued)

wisdom

*How can I allow the L*ORD *to use this Healing Word in my heart and in my life?*

_____
_____
_____
_____
_____
_____
_____
_____
_____
_____
_____
_____
_____
_____
_____
_____
_____
_____
_____
_____
_____
_____
_____
_____
_____
_____
_____
_____

DATE:_____

wisdom...
(continued)

obedience

How can I allow the L{\scriptsize ORD} to use this Healing Word in my heart and in my life?

_____
_____
_____
_____
_____
_____
_____
_____
_____
_____
_____
_____
_____
_____
_____
_____
_____
_____
_____
_____
_____
_____
_____
_____
_____

DATE:_____

obedience...
(continued)

mercy

How can I allow the Lord to use this Healing Word in my heart and in my life?

_____
_____
_____
_____
_____
_____
_____
_____
_____
_____
_____
_____
_____
_____
_____
_____
_____
_____
_____
_____
_____
_____
_____
_____
_____
_____
_____

DATE:_____

mercy...
(continued)

joy

How can I allow the LORD to use this Healing Word in my heart and in my life?

_____
_____
_____
_____
_____
_____
_____
_____
_____
_____
_____
_____
_____
_____
_____
_____
_____
_____
_____
_____
_____
_____
_____
_____
_____
_____

DATE:_____

joy...
(continued)

worship

How can I allow the LORD to use this Healing Word in my heart and in my life?

_____
_____
_____
_____
_____
_____
_____
_____
_____
_____
_____
_____
_____
_____
_____
_____
_____
_____
_____
_____
_____
_____
_____
_____
_____
_____
_____
_____

DATE:_____

worship...
(continued)

holiness

How can I allow the LORD to use this Healing Word in my heart and in my life?

_____
_____
_____
_____
_____
_____
_____
_____
_____
_____
_____
_____
_____
_____
_____
_____
_____
_____
_____
_____
_____
_____
_____
_____
_____
_____
_____
_____

DATE:_____

holiness...
(continued)

confession

*How can I allow the Lord to use this Healing Word in
my heart and in my life?*

_____
_____
_____
_____
_____
_____
_____
_____
_____
_____
_____
_____
_____
_____
_____
_____
_____
_____
_____
_____
_____
_____
_____
_____
_____
_____

DATE:_____

confession...
(continued)

refuge

How can I allow the L<small>ORD</small> to use this Healing Word in my heart and in my life?

_____
_____
_____
_____
_____
_____
_____
_____
_____
_____
_____
_____
_____
_____
_____
_____
_____
_____
_____
_____
_____
_____
_____
_____
_____
_____
_____
_____

DATE:_____

refuge...
(continued)

love

How can I allow the Lord to use this Healing Word in my heart and in my life?

_____
_____
_____
_____
_____
_____
_____
_____
_____
_____
_____
_____
_____
_____
_____
_____
_____
_____
_____
_____
_____
_____
_____
_____

DATE:_____

love...
(continued)

humility

How can I allow the LORD *to use this Healing Word in my heart and in my life?*

_____
_____
_____
_____
_____
_____
_____
_____
_____
_____
_____
_____
_____
_____
_____
_____
_____
_____
_____
_____
_____
_____
_____
_____
_____
_____
_____

DATE:_____

humility...
(continued)

deliverance

*How can I allow the L*ORD *to use this Healing Word in my heart and in my life?*

_____

_____

_____

_____

_____

_____

_____

_____

_____

_____

_____

_____

_____

_____

_____

_____

_____

_____

_____

_____

_____

_____

_____

_____

_____

DATE:_____

deliverance...
(continued)

yielded

How can I allow the Lord *to use this Healing Word in my heart and in my life?*

_____
_____
_____
_____
_____
_____
_____
_____
_____
_____
_____
_____
_____
_____
_____
_____
_____
_____
_____
_____
_____
_____
_____
_____
_____
_____
_____
_____

DATE:_____

yielded...
(continued)

steadfast

How can I allow the LORD to use this Healing Word in my heart and in my life?

_____

_____

_____

_____

_____

_____

_____

_____

_____

_____

_____

_____

_____

_____

_____

_____

_____

_____

_____

_____

_____

_____

_____

_____

_____

_____

DATE:_____

steadfast...
(continued)

balance

How can I allow the L<small>ORD</small> to use this Healing Word in my heart and in my life?

_____

_____

_____

_____

_____

_____

_____

_____

_____

_____

_____

_____

_____

_____

_____

_____

_____

_____

_____

_____

_____

_____

_____

_____

_____

_____

DATE:_____

balance...
(continued)

united

How can I allow the L<small>ORD</small> to use this Healing Word in my heart and in my life?

_____
_____
_____
_____
_____
_____
_____
_____
_____
_____
_____
_____
_____
_____
_____
_____
_____
_____
_____
_____
_____
_____
_____
_____
_____
_____

DATE:_____

united...
(continued)

acceptance

How can I allow the L ORD to use this Healing Word in my heart and in my life?

_____
_____
_____
_____
_____
_____
_____
_____
_____
_____
_____
_____
_____
_____
_____
_____
_____
_____
_____
_____
_____
_____
_____
_____
_____
_____
_____
_____
_____

DATE:_____

acceptance...
(continued)

References

Agnes, Michael, Editor. <u>Webster's New World Dictionary.</u> Cleveland, Ohio: Wiley Publishing, 2003.

Baker, Warren, Editor. <u>The Complete Word Study Old Testament.</u> Chattanooga, Tennessee: AMG Publishers, 1994.

<u>Barnes' Notes.</u> Electronic Database: Biblesoft, 1997.

Brown, Colin, Editor. <u>New International Dictionary of New Testament Theology</u>, Vols. 1-4. Grand Rapids, Michigan: Zondervan, 1986.

<u>Brown-Driver-Briggs Hebrew and English Lexicon.</u> Electronic Database: Biblesoft, 2002.

<u>Clarke's Commentary.</u> Electronic Database: Biblesoft, 1996.

<u>Matthew Henry's Commentary on the Whole Bible.</u> Electronic Database: Hendrickson Publishers, 1991.

Olson, Reuben, et. al. <u>Zondervan NASB Exhaustive Concordance.</u> Grand Rapids, Michigan: Zondervan Publishing House, 1998.

Ryken, Leland, et. al. <u>Dictionary of Biblical Imagery.</u> Downers Grove, Illinois: Intervarsity Press, 1998.

Spangler, Ann. <u>Praying the Names of God.</u> Grand Rapids, Michigan: Zondervan, 2004, pp. 98-100. (Emphasis added)

Strong, James. <u>The New Strong's Exhaustive Concordance of the Bible.</u> Nashville, Tennessee: Thomas Nelson: 1995.

<u>Thayer's Greek Lexicon.</u> Electronic Database: Biblesoft, 2000.

Vine, W., et. al. <u>Vine's Complete Expository Dictionary of Old and New Testament Words.</u> Nashville, Tennessee: Thomas Nelson, 1996.

Wigram, George. <u>The Englishman's Greek Concordance of the New Testament.</u> Peabody, Massachusetts: Hendrickson Publishers, 1999.

Wigram, George. <u>The Englishman's Hebrew Concordance of the Old Testament.</u> Peabody, Massachusetts: Hendrickson Publishers, 2001.

<u>The Wycliffe Bible Commentary.</u> Electronic Database: Moody Press, 1962.

Zodhiates, Spiros, Editor. <u>The Complete Word Study Dictionary: New Testament.</u> Chattanooga, Tennessee: AMG Publishers, 1992.

Zodhiates, Spiros, Editor. <u>The Complete Word Study New Testament with Parallel Greek.</u> Chattanooga, Tennessee: AMG Publishers, 1992.

This book was produced in conjunction with:

HEALING WORD
PSYCHOTHERAPY SERVICES, LLC
Mequon, Wisconsin ♦ www.healing-word.com

Printed in the United States
48378LVS00007B/67-117